FOR WHAT IT'S WORTH

A Guide for New Stockbrokers

by

Eugene A. Kelly

Marshwinds
Advisory Company

Copies of the book may be obtained
by sending $19.95 to:
    Marshwinds Advisory Company
    P.O. Box 3204
    Thomasville, Georgia 31799

Georgia residents add 4% sales tax.

ISBN 0-9614496-0-8

Library of Congress Catalog Number 85-60051

First Printing . . . . March 1985
Second Printing . . . . August 1985
Third Printing . . . . November 1985

for

Judy Carolyn

and

David Justin

as well as

Special remembrance of

Eula Waters Aaron

1910–1985

TABLE OF CONTENTS

THE BIG PICTURE

CHALKLINES

BUILDING A BOOK

SALESMANSHIP

MAKING MONEY

KEEPING IT TOGETHER

ABOUT THIS BOOK

First, masculine pronouns are used when speaking of brokers and clients and feminine pronouns are used when speaking of sales assistants. No prejudice or slight is intended. None should be taken.

The column "MY WAY" is there because there is no *one* correct way to do business. The purpose of the book is to stimulate the reader to think about the topics contained herein, to formulate ideas, and to develop his own style of accomplishment. Ultimately, the professional level of service rendered by the entire industry can be improved in this way.

Preface

I have wanted to write this book since 1968 when I first became interested in being a stock-broker. At that time I thought I could find a book which would give me an indication of what the job was about and how to enter the field. I was wrong.

There is very little written about the field, and what is written deals with "How" in a limited fashion but not "Why." This book tries to do both. Training classes will give mechanics; this book attempts to give understanding. Its size is the same as a "Holding Page" book. This was done on purpose.

The young stockbroker, now called a Financial Consultant, should use this book as a daily reference guide. Each FWIW is written assuming the reader is a new stockbroker.

Notice I said reference guide, not answer book. Our business is one where success comes in many individualistic ways. The reader of this book will quickly find a FWIW which he does not agree with. For that reader, my approach will not work. This is why I left the "MY WAY" column for notes. Each reader should use my approach as a starting point and adapt his own successful meth-on to achieve his goal.

The overall objective of this book is to enhance the professionalism of our industry. Those of us who are fortunate enough to be in this business are truly blessed. We owe it to ourselves, our families, our clients, and our own personal GOD to bring to our career a level of professionalism which inspires those we come in contact with.

There are many who could have done a better job of writing this book—bigger producers and better managers—but they did not. I did. In sales nothing is original. Due to publication permission restrictions, I can not recognize some of those who influenced some of the material.

If the book is a success it will achieve my objective. If not, perhaps it will cause someone to write a better book. If so, my objective will also be achieved. Either way the public's interest is served.

Special credit needs to be given to Florence C. Smyth, (CopyWrite Savannah, Georgia), who took the second draft of the manuscript and did an unbelievable job in correcting my use of the English language. Rencie gets the credit for the book being readable. Where poor grammar is used, it's my fault for not following her suggestions.

Finally, a word about my wife, Judy. Her contribution to this work is as great as mine. She encouraged me, she put up with my frustrations and she typed and reviewed each of the drafts. Judy is my confidant and sounding board. There is no question this book would not have made it to publication without her assistance.

Eugene A. Kelly

November 25, 1984   Midway, Georgia

THE BIG
PICTURE

MY WAY

The Random House College Dictionary defines an entrepreneur as "a person who organizes, manages, and assumes responsiblity for a business or other enterprise." Generally, an entrepreneur is thought to be someone who owns and operates a grocery store, wholesale business, small manufacturing business, or restaurant and employs people. Stockbrokers are thought of as employees, not employers, and never as entrepreneurs. But this is a misconception. A comparison of a small retail merchant and a stockbroker will illustrate the similarities between the two.

The merchant has gross sales from which his cost of goods sold is deducted to obtain his gross margin. From the gross margin selling and administrative expenses are deducted to arrive at his profit before taxes. Generally, this figure is 10% to 20% of sales. After deducting income taxes the merchant has net income after taxes, usually 5% to 10% of sales.

Now let's look at the stockbroker. He has gross commissions from his dealings with the public, which are his "sales." In essence, he contracts with the firm of his choice for certain services the same way a merchant buys merchandise from selected vendors. The cost of these services, usually 50% to 70% of "sales", is the broker's gross margin. Additional selling and administrative costs that the broker chooses to incur are deducted from this gross margin. These might include a bonus for his sales assistant, a subscription to a chart service, or a personal computer set up. Whatever they are, the additional expenditures are discretionary. Therefore, the broker's net before taxes can run up to 50% of "sales", with the general norm being 35%. This is

3

MY WAY

100% to 200% more than that of the retail merchant! (The reader can choose any business or industry he likes, but he will find it hard to come up with one which has a net income before taxes of 35%.)

One response to this analogy is that the broker does not build net worth through retained earnings like the business man does. While this is true, it is by choice or ignorance, and not by the nature of the business. Any business owner has the opportunity to draw a salary as well as keep the net profits after taxes. The stockbroker has the same choice. He can spend all of his income or invest a portion as "retained earnings". As a matter of fact, his "retained earnings" have the advantage of being in the form of marketable securities which offer him liquidity, which is denied to small businessmen who reinvest their retained earnings in their own business.

The best advantage the stockbroker has over the entrepreneur is the amount of capital it takes him to begin his business. A fast food franchise requires $200,000 or more just to begin. A retail merchant's available capital for inventory directly determines his potential sales. A small manufacturer must finance inventory and receivables as well as plant facilities. On the other hand, the stockbroker needs nothing. Through his association with his firm, the broker is able to begin doing business without any extra capital. His personal efforts and integrity are all that is necessary to enter the business.

Finally, few businesses offer individuals from every walk of life easy access and the opportunity to become some of the highest paid professionals in their local community as well as in the nation as a whole. The "business" of being a stockbroker does just that. The broker only needs patience,

4

persistance, and desire to be successful. He is truly an entrepreneur.

FWIW # 2 .... Equity Capital

While a stockbroker does not have to have any capital other than "sweat" equity, he should go a step further by making some monetary contributions to his new enterprise. He should sit down after completing his training and ask himself what is needed to get the job done. Clothes? A Club Membership? A Personal Computer? Chart Subscriptions? Motivational Training? He should take a complete inventory of everything that needs to be acquired and go out and do it. The expenditures are investments in himself and his future. The new broker is what he perceives himself to be and nothing more. If the broker is not professional in every respect, he will know it no matter how well he manages to fool others.

The question is, how does he get the money to invest when he is just starting out? The answer is, he should borrow it. Every bank in the country and every major credit card company is willing to extend to the public a personal line of credit. The new broker can get a Visa *and* Mastercharge with a $750.00 credit line on each for a total of $1,500.00. He can spend the money in the following manner:

The broker's personal appearance is foremost on his inventory. (This subject will be dealt with in greater detail later. See FWIW # 8.) The young broker should allocate two/thirds of his new credit line to clothes for the office. An aside is warranted here. FWIW # 8 advocates buying only the best. This poses a problem for the young

MY WAY

broker who is starting out on a salary that is inadequate for sustaining his family, much less for buying expensive clothes. At this point in his career he may need to compromise a bit. The broker's main emphasis should be on looking neat and professional. As his career progresses, he can work on looking prosperous as well.

The new broker should invest the remaining money in furthuring his professional education. He should subscribe to publications and start a professional library. Going to the public library won't work. He should buy the books. All kinds of books dealing with the stock market, investments and salesmanship. He should buy cassettes on motivation. The broker should own his library because he will constantly be learning new concepts and features that will unlock puzzles in his head and allow him to reread books and articles with new insight.

Finally, every broker should have his own chart service. Which one he chooses depends upon the type of business he does and his level of knowledge. Clothes and education should cost $1,500.00. The young broker should pay the interest monthly and should be able to pay off the principal from his adjusted compensation checks by the end of the year.

As the broker matures and his business grows, he will need to invest more capital in it, just as he would in any growing business. Sooner or later a broker needs to make a decision on a personal computer or dictating equipment. And eventually he must decide if he should begin to pay for a registered sales assistant. If he earns a private office he will have to decide whether to furnish the whole place himself. All of these decisions are personal and require some capital to implement.

What the young broker needs to understand is that any growing business consumes capital and that his is no different.

MY WAY

FWIW # 3 .... Time Investment

Some successful stockbrokers will advise new trainees to work long and hard hours. Others will tell them to work smart. The fact is, a young broker probably does not know enough to work smart and therefore needs to work long and hard hours to figure out how to get ahead. Managers tell young brokers to make 40 or 50 calls per day, including Saturday. This is supposed to be the secret of success. If so, why do so many young brokers who do it fail?

One of the misguiding precepts of our society is that if a person tries hard enough, long enough and often enough, he will be rewarded. Unfortunately that is not true in the brokerage business. *There is no reward for trying; only for succeeding.* From the beginning, therefore, the young broker must consciously cultivate habits which lead to success. He should work out his day not as a new broker with a few clients, but as an experienced broker whose client book is full. A suggested work day for a young broker who lives within a 25 minute drive of his office is as follows. A broker who must take a train, subway, or bus can make adjustments, but should still make certain each function is performed.

MY WAY | WEEKDAYS:

6:00a.m. - 6:45a.m. - Shower and dress.

6:45a.m. - 7:30a.m. - Read the local paper and have breakfast.

7:30a.m. - 8:00a.m. - Travel to Office; listen to cassettes.

8:00a.m. - 9:00a.m. - Read WSJ and market information if appointment is unavailable.

9:00a.m. - 12: noon - Appointments in office; call prospects/clients.

12: noon . - 1:00p.m. - Lunch appointment with prospects/clients.

1:00p.m. - 4:00p.m. - Appointments in office; call prospects/clients.

4:00p.m. - 5:00p.m. - Appointments out of office.

5:00p.m. - 6:00p.m. - Return to office; plan next day; clean desk.

6:00p.m. - 6:30p.m. - Travel home; Listen to cassettes.

6:30p.m. - 9:00p.m. - Spend time with family, no work, exercise.

9:00p.m. - 10:00p.m. - Read material on investing.

10:00p.m. - 11:00p.m. - Read material on salesmanship.

SATURDAYS AND HOLIDAYS:

The broker should find two hours each Saturday and holiday to spend one hour reading about investments and one hour reading about salesmanship and presentation. He does not need to work on Sunday if he sticks to his schedule during the rest of the week.

If the foregoing schedule is maintained, the totals are as follows:

Active hours in pros-
pect/client contact: 5 days x 9 hrs. - 45 hrs.
Active hours in acquir-
ing investment know-
ledge: 6 days x 1 hrs. - 6 hrs.
Active hours in acquir-
ing salesmanship skills: 6 days x 1 hrs. - 6 hrs.
                                            _____
                                            57 hrs.

There is no question that a broker can succeed by following the above schedule if he is goal oriented. In addition, the broker will not neglect his health and family, and he will gain in self confidence as he augments all aspects of his business knowledge.

FWIW # 4 .... Love It or Leave It

Most successful brokers are addicted to the business. After six months a young broker should know if he will be able to take the emotional swings which are part of the stock brokerage business. There is no middle ground in this business. The broker is either on top of the emotional

MY WAY

peak, deep in the valley of depression, or in the process of jumping from one to the other.

To be able to progress and to keep his wits about him, the young broker must be able to thrive in this environment and see it as a series of great opportunities rather than grave perils. Because the broker cannot control the environment in which he works, the emotional buffeting he takes actually becomes a pyschological necessity. Each individual has his own level of tolerance for humdrum activity. In stockbrokers, this tolerance level is low. Generally they will seek out recreational hobbies which give them emotional "highs" of competition, uncertainty, risk, and intensity. Inevitably, the typical broker on vacation becomes restless and calls the office before his vacation is over.

FWIW # 5 .... Market Widow

A successful broker is hard to live with. His wife deserves a medal for just being there. Because the broker's life revolves around the market and his emotional states reflect its vicissitudes, his wife is subjected to dramatic, and sometimes traumatic, mood swings. In other words, the market gets the best of him, and his wife gets the rest of him. Often, the broker's wife is at a loss to understand why her husband behaves the way he does. Unless she is very perceptive, she sees only that he is being difficult and unreasonable The scenario goes something like this:

The broker arrives home. His wife is glad to see him, and greets him cheerfully. She is bubbling with news about her day. He is glum and morose.

She tries to brighten his mood first by asking him to tell her what happened (he doesn't want to talk about it) and then makes matters worse by making light of the situation (he is sure that it is the worst thing that has ever happened to anybody). He is short-tempered and sarcastic with her. She soon becomes impatient and irritable with him. He snaps at her and hurts her feelings. She bursts into tears or yells back at him. Whether or not an apology follows, the evening is ruined. Both husband and wife feel misunderstood and sore. Both sulk and suffer in silence.

What the broker cannot or will not bring himself to tell his wife is that he was out of the office when a prospect he had been cultivating for many months telephoned, asking that he return the call. By the time the receptionist gave the broker the message and he got back to his prospect, it was after 4:00 p.m. The prospect proceeded to inform the broker that, due to his apparent lack of interest, he had just opened an account with a competing broker and purchased $1,000,000 worth of municipal bonds with a $25,000 commission. The broker is far too busy kicking himself and cursing his rotten luck to realize or to care that it is unfair to take it out on his wife.

What he wants (and can't have) is another chance at the missed opportunity. What she wants (and can't have) is for her husband to be a nice, even-tempered, easy-going guy who comes home ready to listen to what she has to say.

During calm periods, and preferably before he has completed his training, the young broker should try to warn his spouse about the mood swings which "come with the territory." He may want to give her some reading material to help her become knowledgeable about the brokerage busi-

MY WAY

11

MY WAY

ness. If he has a good day, he should go home primed to cater to his wife's emotional needs. If he does so, she may find it a little easier to cope with his behavior after he has had a bad day.

The experienced market widow knows that any highly lucrative business is also highly stressful, and the brokerage business is no exception. She has learned that when something goes wrong, it is often due to error or neglect on the broker's part. She realizes that in order for him to explain to her what happened, he would probably have to admit to stupidity or carelessness, and that pressing for details is equivalent to asking him to rub salt into an open wound. If her initial probe brings an abrupt or evasive response; the wise market widow drops the subject. She leaves her husband alone and gives him time to get over the situation.

FWIW # 6 .... The Habit of Winning

Vince Lombardi once said that winning was a habit, and so was losing. Earl Nightengale made a recording about how successful people make a habit of doing the things failures don't want to do. The young broker must realize that both good and bad habits are easy to form and hard to break. The world is full of losers and failures who could have been winners and successes if they had had the self-discipline to form good habits. Some of them even delude themselves into thinking they could still do it if they really wanted to. The young broker must not kid himself. If he wants to be one of life's few success stories, he has to make a habit of conducting each and every aspect of his life as a winner, and he should start immediately.

When people are young they tend to believe that they have all the time in the world, and that they can perfect a skill as easily and as quickly as they can turn on a spigot. They get by in school by "cramming" for tests at the last minute instead of studying regularly. They believe that they can do the same in their business careers and still get ahead. This is a fallacy.

It is a fallacy because the brokerage business is built on human relationships, and these take time to develop. When a stockbroker asks a prospect or a client for an order, he is asking him to entrust him with something very precious - his money. It is the rare prospect or client who will commit a large sum of money to a broker's stewardship unless he has been doing business with him for some time and thinks he knows him pretty well. Good clients can take as long as three or four years to "develop" and make "profitable." While the prospect and the broker are in the process of establishing their relationship, the prospect will deal with the broker when he is in high spirits and when he is feeling low. The broker must never allow his own emotional state to affect his dealings with his prospects and clients. He must establish the practice of performing his duties in a professional manner at all times, regardless of his mood. Every time he does so, the broker will strengthen his ability to suppress his frustrations automatically, and this in turn will confirm people's perceptions of him as being strong, stable, and unflappable. His continued professional conduct will bring him more business and greater success, thus dissipating his frustrations.

The young broker can form the winning habit of doing what failures don't want to do by tackling whatever task is at hand, no matter how dis-

MY WAY

MY WAY

tasteful, in a professional manner and to the best of his ability. By never allowing himself to "let up" or "slack off." By giving it 100%. By taking a few minutes each night to reflect upon today's accomplishments and tomorrow's challenges. By leaving nothing to "luck" or to "chance." By being cheerful, up-beat, calm, and even-tempered. By thinking positively. By remembering that success consists not of one great battle, but of a series of small daily victories.

FWIW # 7 .... The Fire Within

"He's dedicated." "He's hungry." "He's a killer." "He's determined." "He's a worker/workaholic." "He's ambitious." "He won't take 'no' for an answer." People have made all of these pronouncements at one time or another in their attempts to characterize a successful stockbroker. All are correct, but none is comprehensive. Each declaration represents an effort to "put a finger on" the intangible quality which makes anyone successful in his chosen profession. This impalpable quality is like a person's soul: it is there, and it radiates heat and light, yet it is invisible and indefinable. It is possible neither to create it nor to acquire it. Everyone is born with it, the fire within, but society has decreed that it is uncivilized and dangerous and needs to be extinguished. And so most people spend their lives banking it in the ashes of conventional behavior so that they, too, will be deemed nice, polite, upright citizens.

When society fails to compensate a person for putting out his inner fire, and when the satisfaction of selling provides the fuel to rekindle the embers, the blaze begins to burn brightly. Society, envious of such a person's success, is quick to label him as aggressive and unscrupulous, but he no longer cares about its approval or its jealousy.

When asked to what he attributes his success, such a person replies, "Well, I'm not sure. I just do whatever is necessary to get the job done."

As the young stockbroker begins his career, it is important for him to avoid people who would smother his inner fire with a wet blanket, and to seek out people who will add fuel to the fire, who will fan the flames and allow them to burn unchecked and unhindered.

MY WAY

FWIW # 8 .... Book Cover

People are taught at an early age that "you can't judge a book by its cover." Yet, that is exactly what 95% of them do! People who encounter a man who is shabbily dressed and unshaven tend to write him off as a person of no importance. If a person sees a man with a "loud" tie, wrinkled shirt, scuffed shoes, or shaggy hair, the observer is less likely to think he is successful than if he is dressed in a tailored suit, white shirt, conservative tie, polished shoes, and has hair which is neatly cut and combed. The manner in which a man wears his clothes is as important in setting his image as what he wears.

A young stockbroker does not want people to remember what he was wearing, just how he looked. Everyone has certain sterotypical images of what should be worn by people in all occupations. If a young stockbroker looks like his prospect/client thinks he should look, at most the prospect/client will have relaxed and secure feelings, and at least will not have uncomfortable and

MY WAY

suspicious feelings. To make a good initial impression is to make it past the first barrier without setting off an alarm. This awareness on the part of the client may be completely subliminal, but, if asked, he should be able to respond: "Well, he looks like a stockbroker ought to look."

The problem with looking the way a stockbroker is suppose to look is that the "right" look will vary from locale to locale. In a resort community the appropriate dress code may be a sport shirt and slacks. In a small town, a dress shirt, sport coat and slacks are acceptable. In a big city, only a business suit and tie will suffice. For most brokers, the business suit is the proper dress. A young broker should look around him and determine what it will take for him to stand out slightly as being a cut above his competition. The broker who habitually wears a sport coat and who shows up in a suit only on a day when he has a meeting with an important client betrays his low opinion of the rest of his clients. Every day should be important enough for him to look his best. What frame of mind is he in when he does not look his best? Probably not as sharp as when he knows he is dressed properly. A broker should look his best each and every day no matter what appointments he has that day.

Is it OK for a broker to take his coat off in the office? Over 90% of brokers do, particularly those in a "bull pen," and most clients accept the practice. There is nothing wrong with wearing shirt sleeves in the office, but if all of the other brokers in the boardroom have their coats off, won't the broker who has his on make a better impression on clients?

When buying clothes for the office, the young broker should set out to purchase a complete wardrobe. He should take someone with him whom he trusts to help match colors and styles. The wardrobe should consist of the following:

(1) 5 suits - All wool (light weight in the South) - navy or gray tones, and of a conservative cut.
(2) 10 white shirts - All cotton or poly-cotton blend.
(3) 2 pairs - Black shoes.
(4) Black socks.
(5) 10 silk ties.
(6) Black belt with custom buckle.
(7) Gold ring/watch/cuff links.
(8) White handkerchiefs for breast pocket.
(9) Wool overcoat for winter.
(10) Black umbrella.

Brown and green tones in business suits are not as acceptable as navy and grey tones. The fabric should be all wool in as fine a quality as the young broker can afford. He should have one suit for every day of the business week. This way the suits will only be worn once a week and should last for some time. Since few young people can afford to purchase five suits at a time, a schedule of purchasing one every six months will give the new broker a complete complement in 2½ years. After that, the useable suits should be maintained at five.

If the oldest suit is still serviceable, the broker should wear it when the environment could be harsh on a suit. Upon arriving home, the broker should remove his suit and hang it on a shaped, wooden hanger. The suits should not be dry cleaned too frequently. Under normal circumstances, twice a quarter should be satisfactory.

MY WAY

Finally, the suits should be a conservative cut which will remain in style over several fashion cycles.

In selecting shirts, the broker can make a personal choice between a button-down collar and a traditional collar, and between french cuffs and cuffs with buttons. Light blue shirts are considered as acceptable as white shirts in most areas. However, a sparkling crisp white shirt has greater impact.

When purchasing business shoes, the young broker should purchase two pairs. He should get some shoe trees and use them daily in order to extend the life of the shoes. These shoes should be the most expensive the broker can afford. They should be conservative as well. It is necessary to have two pairs so that one can dry out while the other is being worn. Of course, the shoes should be polished at all times. Finally, the broker should wear black over-the-calf length socks.

Female brokers have the same requirements to dress properly as their male counterparts. If anything, the pressure is for them to even look more the part. A delicate balance between looking professional and looking feminine is needed. A woman cannot be a man, and, therefore, should not attempt to look like one. No one expects her to.

A suit is the most appropriate attire for a woman in business. As with a man, the color tones should be navy or gray. Along with the suit should be a blouse with a neckline which is just that - a neckline. Bows or scarfs lend a nice feminine, yet professional, look. Closed pumps are the only appropriate shoe for the young female broker.

Finally, the professional woman's clothes should fit properly. Blouses which gap open detract from her professionalism. Skirts should fit properly and the hemline should be mid-knee or lower.

The broker can express his individuality in his choice of ties. Bright colors are permissible as long as the ties are not "flashy." If he selects two ties for each suit, the broker will not have to wear the same one twice in a two week period. As important as the tie itself is the way in which it is worn. The tie should reach to the top of the belt buckle, and there should not be a gap between the tie and the belt.

The broker's belt should be a fine quality black leather strap with a tasteful gold or silver buckle which reflects the image protrayed. The broker's jewelry can quietly reflect his personality. A ring, a watch, or cuff links that are distinctive without being vulgar can also shape the broker's presence. A man who lets his wife pick out these personal items forfeits the opportunity to have his own taste reflected in his jewelry. A snow white handkerchief in the suit's breast pocket also adds distinction.

For the winter months, the broker should get a good wool overcoat and a nice wide umbrella. The coat should be solid black, gray, or herringbone tweed while the umbrella should also be black with a distinctive handle.

Finally, a matter of common sense. It would be impossible for a young man who is trying to raise a family or buy a house to purchase this complete wardrobe all at once. The young broker should take an inventory of what he has that is good, rank his priorities for completing the wardrobe, and fill in the missing pieces on a regularly

MY WAY

19

MY WAY

scheduled basis. His appearance will assist him in having the proper outlook and presence for his success.

FWIW # 9 ....Specialist vs. Generalist

Ever since there have been brokers, they have argued about whether it is better to be a specialist or generalist. Interestingly, there are enough successful brokers of both persuasions to ensure that the argument is not going to be settled at any time in the near future. One thing is certain: the young broker should not make the decision until he has been in the business for at least three years. It is not until a broker has actually acquired experience in all areas of investing that he can know for sure what area naturally attracts him. He must get a feeling for his sales territory to know what area gives him the widest range of opportunities.

Terminology needs to be defined. In 1973, a "specialist" was someone who dealt in commodities, OTC stocks, government bonds, or tax shelters. Today a "specialist" is someone who deals in equities, fixed income, or financial planning. These are much broader categories reflecting the greater diversification of financial assets.

Just because a broker is a "specialist" in some area does not mean that he cannot deal in all kinds of investments. It means that he chooses to "concentrate" his prospecting and business in one particular class of investments. Because he becomes an "expert" in one area, the broker is able to improve his prospecting techniques and, thereby, increase his ability to gather assets. Once the client is on the books, the broker can take care of all of his investment needs.

MY WAY

It is human nature to seek out the reputed expert in any given field, whether it's medicine, law or automobile repair. People admire a "specialist" and feel they are getting additional expertise by going to him.

There is another aspect as well. A broker who takes the time to really become knowledgeable in one investment area gains appreciably in self-confidence, and this is conveyed through his sales presentation. A better sales presentation translates into more accounts and more business.

A final element of the "specialist" psychology is the halo effect: even if a prospect's/client's particular interest lies in another area of investments, he will generally trust the broker's judgment in that area because of the confidence generated by his expertise in his area of specialization. In other words, the shining light of expertise casts a glow that extends beyond the area of primary illumination.

An area of expertise should meet the following criteria:

(1) A large number of investors have an interest in it.
(2) There is price volatility for capital gains potential.
(3) The area is complex and therefore requires extensive study and research.
(4) The cost of the investment is not prohibitive.
(5) Turnover of assets is possible.

FWIW # 10 .... Keys to Success

Many a young broker thinks that prospecting is the only key to success in the brokerage business.

MY WAY

He is told that if he opens 250 + accounts each year for the first three years, he will have it made. In reality, the typical young broker will have a total of only ±200 accounts after completing his first three years—if he survives that long. Even after opening large numbers of new accounts, many young brokers never even make it to the third year due to lack of production. When reassigning their accounts, their managers will wonder how or why these young brokers failed with as much potential as their accounts indicate. Upon close scrutiny, the reason becomes apparent. The young brokers failed because they emphasized one aspect of the business, prospecting, to the exclusion of the other two: salesmanship and investment knowledge.

Prospecting is clearly the first requirement for success in the brokerage business. An entire section of this book is devoted to the subject. Suffice it to say that prospecting must be done regularly and consistently in order to be effective.

Salesmanship is the second key to success. Contrary to popular belief, salesmen are made, not born. To put it another way, salesmanship is a product of environment rather than heredity. A desire to succeed is an essential component of the salesman's make-up. Just having the desire, however, is not enough to ensure success. The young broker must learn and practice good salesmanship. He must master the skills of salesmanship since selling is part art and part science. Behavioral psychology has made great advances in identifying and improving effective communication techniques, and communication is what selling is all about. Unless the salesman has sharpened and polished his communication skills, he cannot discover the wants and needs of the prospect, never mind satisfy them. Each and every day, therefore, the young broker should conscientiously work on the communication skills necessary to upgrade his sales presentations by studying material on the subject of selling. He should develop and refine two or three scripts to determine which one is the most effective. He should study and restudy the anatomy of the sales presentation until it becomes second nature for him to think and talk in a sales-oriented fashion. The young broker should practice methods of asking probing questions in a subtle, non-offensive manner. This is much harder to do than it sounds. Getting people to tell the truth about their financial circumstances is about as easy as getting them to speak openly and honestly about their sex lives. If salesmanship was easy to master, its rewards would not be so great. Salesmanship is a set of skills acquired like any other: through practice, practice, and more practice, and by learning from mistakes so that they are not repeated.

The third key to success is investment knowledge. The young broker must implement a planned program of broadening and deeping his investment knowledge. He should expand his knowledge carefully and deliberately and in an organized manner so that he retains what he has studied and can put it to use daily. The young broker should start with an overview of the securities business in order to learn about relationships and how they interact. Once he understands "the big picture," he can focus on individual investment vehicles in order to learn more about each security. Throughout his studies, the young broker should verify the fact that there are plenty of prospects in his sales territory who could benefit from the investments under scrutiny. There

MY WAY

MY WAY

is so much to be learned that he cannot afford the luxury of developing expertise in an investment area with only limited application.

The young broker should spend at least one hour a day, six days a week studying salesmanship, and the same amount of time studying investments. He should devote about 45 hours a week to prospecting. It is impossible to predict how well a broker who meets these requirements for success will do, but any young broker who does not make it a practice to work regularly and hard on all three is guaranteed to fail.

FWIW # 11 . . . Nice to Know vs. Need to Know

One of the things that shocks the young broker is the astounding amount of pertinent information which is available to him every day. If he tried to read every bit of it he wouldn't get anything done. The young broker must decide what to read. This is how he does it. He separates his material into two categories: (1) "Nice to know" and (2) "Need to know" information. The natural tendency is to read the "Nice to know" information first because it is more entertaining. To further complicate matters, material keeps moving from one category to another, as circumstances change.

If a major prospect/client reads a certain business magazine religiously, the broker must put that magazine on his "need to know" list. Few things detract from a smooth relationship more than a client's wanting to discuss an article the broker has not read. Some clients read alot of "scare" articles and other emotionally distorted material that should not influence the decision-making process. The broker needs to skim such material and read plenty of reliable information as well. Only by "getting the facts" from a number of different sources can he begin to develop the judgement to make intelligent investment decisions. If a broker learns to separate fact from opinion, he will grow.

FWIW # 12 .... **Clients vs. Customers**

Retail stores, fast food chains, automobile dealers and other service businesses have *customers*. Professionals have *clients*. A stockbroker has *clients*.

FWIW # 13 ......**Why People Use Full Service Brokers**

Discount brokers do not really understand why the overwhelming majority of the investing public uses full service brokers at twice the price. The reason has to do with the fact that only a few people are capable of preserving their capital, much less adding to it. Skillful investing cannot be accomplished by reading a newspaper for twenty minutes a day. Investors turn to full service brokers for guidance in preserving their capital and adding to it because discount brokers are merely "order takers," and not advisors. Every young broker should realize that he will always have a clientele to serve if he becomes knowledgeable in the major areas of his business.

MY WAY

MY WAY

FWIW # 14 ..... Clients with Multiple Brokers

Everyone likes to be the one and only. It is only natural to feel possessive about objects and people that one values. The broker would like to believe that he can woo his prospects/clients away from any other brokers they may be using. Some brokers even take this egotism to the dangerous point of feeling slighted or betrayed if their clients continue to use other brokers. Such a broker should stop and consider the situation for a moment. Of course it would be nice to capture all of a client's assets, but, if he can't do that, the broker should have enough confidence in his own professionalism to at least become the dominant advisor to the client. If the client already had another broker, and he opened a second account elsewhere, he obviously must have thought the second broker offered something that the first did not. The second broker should take advantage of the situation by letting the client know that he stands ready to discuss and review any investment idea presented to the client by the first broker or anyone else. Over time, the client will come to depend upon the second broker more and more.

Finally, a professional broker's competence will be accentuated when compared with the performance of his competitors. This "sharing" of clients, like any competitive situation, should keep the broker on his toes and motivate him to be better at his chosen career.

FWIW # 15 .... 80/20 Rule

One of the interesting rules of thumb of the brokerage business is that 80% of a broker's business comes from 20% of his accounts. This holds true for the $200,000 producer as well as for the $500,000 producer. It raises some interesting points. First of all, it should be evident to each new broker that he had better find some larger, active accounts. With the emphasis on prospecting for a large number of new accounts, the young broker sometimes loses sight of his ultimate real objective. With a goal of 250 new accounts each year in mind, quality sometimes is sacrificed for quantity. The young broker who will keep quality foremost in mind will begin to recognize the high quality prospect and the fact that he is probably already the client of another broker. This is when salesmanship comes into the picture. Patience, persistence, and probing questions are part of the process of capturing these potentially important accounts.

Common sense should tell the broker that if he lands a high quality account, he should seek out the new client's friends and associates. Birds of a feather do flock together, and active participants in the stock market do talk about the market with their peers.

Since the 80/20 Rule seems to hold true for all sizes of producers, it follows that the only difference between a $200,000 and a $500,000 producer is the desire and the ability to "capture" more large accounts. This means that the larger producer does not reduce his prospecting as he opens more accounts. Instead, he improves his organizational skills, shifts his prospecting from a shotgunning to a rifling approach, begins to actively manage his sales assistant, and asks for larger orders.

Finally, each year a broker should review his revenue breakdown by account and cull from his

MY WAY

MY WAY

book the bottom 20% of his accounts if they offer limited potential.

FWIW # 16 ....Client vs. Prospect

Prospecting is hard. Most young brokers fail because they either do not want to prospect or they think they do not have to prospect. Most good accounts, ($1,000 or more in commissions), are opened only after repeated contacts and months of work. Knowing he must woo the prospect until he wins him as a client, the broker puts his best foot forward during the courtship. Then what happens? Having made his conquest, he heaves a sigh of relief and, in some cases, he neglects his new client! The broker treats the client as if he were a possession that could not leave. Yet, when former clients are questioned about why they closed their accounts they cite "too busy," "indifferent" and "no service" as major causes of their desertion. All of the time and effort devoted to winning the trust and confidence of the prospect is wasted because of the broker's less than professional attitude. Some brokers seem to lose sight of the value that a client has over a prospect as time goes on. The broker who consciously calculates the level of service given to each client and utilizes his sales assistant properly in developing his broker/client relationships will be able to retain more of his clients for longer periods. By keeping more clients longer and continuing to prospect, a broker will build a substantial book. Simple, isn't it? In short, the way a broker increases his production is by getting more clients, by getting more commissions from each client, or a combination of the two. Since getting more commissions from each client must be done within the framework of a client's investment objectives, and getting new clients requires long weeks and months of prospecting, a young broker should never lose sight of the value a client has over a prospect. There is no question that an existing client is easier to service and keep happy than it is to get a new one.

MY WAY

FWIW # 17 .... Six Month Blues

When an outsider is asked to talk about what he thinks a stockbroker does for a living, he usually describes someone whose day consists of the Wall Street Journal, answering a few calls from clients, taking a long lunch hour, and finishing off the day playing golf at his club. Even the young trainee observing the older, established brokers in his office sees people who don't seem to do much more than read, talk on the phone and write orders. As his training progresses, the trainee's expectations of success begin to build because he *knows* he is going to be more creative and more dedicated than the brokers he sees around him. His energy and enthusiasm rise to fever pitch as, in the artificial atmosphere of the training class, he develops sales scripts full of sure-fire logic no prospect could possibly resist.

Reality begins to intrude upon the young broker's fantasy life during his first week in production. He does not know how to pace himself, and, as his energy level drains along with his expectations of fast success, the neophyte begins to doubt his firm's research ability, the firm's ability to provide service, and his own ability to

MY WAY

be a broker. The young broker is beginning to find out just how difficult it is to be a stockbroker. He has begun to experience the "six month blues". The young broker is realizing that the glamour he thought the business offered is not there. He is finding out that success is 1% inspiration and 99% perspiration.

The young broker experiencing the "six month blues" should stop and take a look around the boardroom. In doing so, he will realize that in most cases, he is as smart, as smooth, and as good looking as any broker there. If he has the "want to", he will shed all of his preconceived ideas and illusions and get down to business. He will begin to ask intelligent questions. He will spend time on all three necessary activities - prospecting, selling, and acquiring investment knowledge. He will take inventory of his present clients and begin again.

Young brokers who have survived the "six month blues" will have a great deal more humility and determination. Their love of the business will grow. Best of all, these budding professionals will begin to achieve success both psychologically and financially.

FWIW # 18 .... **Adaptability**

Adaptable is a word which is often used to describe a professional stockbroker. While he must do a great deal of planning in his job, he usually finds that the execution of the plan is difficult. This difficulty stems from the nature of his work, and his mistaken belief that he must handle all aspects of his business personally. Even a broker who has learned to delegate to his sales assistant has problems sticking to his daily plans when his best client calls at 10:00 a.m. demanding an immediate resolution of a problem. While he is working to solve the problem, the time he planned to spend selling and prospecting evaporates.

A young broker with few clients may plan 40 phone calls for the day and find out he can only complete 6 because no one answers on the other 34. Or he may find one call takes 40 minutes because the prospect wants to talk about budget deficits or the gold market. Unless he is adaptable, the broker's stress level will climb as the day goes on.

The area in which a broker must show the most adaptability is in his investment strategy. Suppose there is a period of time during which the most advantageous purchases for his clients are in fixed income investments. Even though the broker may be an equity specialist, he must figure out a way to do what is right for the clients and at the same time keep his business on track, which in this case means finding the right situations in the fixed income area. For an equity specialist, the "right situation" may be convertible securities. Paradoxically, the more detailed his planning, and the more painstaking his implementation of his plan, the more adaptable the broker becomes.

As every broker knows, reality and his daily plan conflict more often than they coincide. Yet, without the daily plan, the broker will not be able to put himself back on track if his attention is diverted by a crisis or a string of "no answers" on the phone. More important, his ability to anticipate and adapt to changes in the investment markets will keep his business growing when his competition is falling behind.

MY WAY

31

MY WAY

FWIW # 19 . . . . . Broker/Manager Relationship

It is commonly known in the business that 90% of the brokers who switch firms do so because of poor relationships with their office managers. A precise study would probably find that 90% is a conservative estimate. Where the relationship between the broker and the manager is one of mutual respect, the chance of the broker's leaving, even when offered up-front money, is greatly reduced due to his dependence on the manager's support. Developing such a healthy relationship is difficult for many reasons, particularly in cases where the manager hired the broker and still tends to see him with all of the faults he had as a trainee. In other cases, a new manager is assigned to an office and has a genuine personality clash with one or more of the established, successful brokers. Some managers have a way of destroying broker loyalty by making them feel as if they are only production numbers. "Produce or get out," and "be good or be gone," are just two of the sayings which have become cliches in the brokerage business. Some managers even feel that new brokers should be given no help or direction since this is a "self-starting" business, and since they received none when they were rookies. Finally, some managers are just plain intimidating and not easily approachable.

How does a young broker develop a good relationship with his manager? First, the young broker should take a few moments to reflect on the manager's personal style. If the manager hired him it is easier since they talked at length during the interview process. If he has been trained under the manager, the young broker has had time to adjust to the manager's ways. What kind

of information does the manager discuss at meet- | *MY WAY*
ings? Where does he place his investment emphasis? What kinds of standards does he set? How
does he allocate perks? These are some of the
behaviors which shed light upon the personality
and style of the manager. While the same questions have to be answered if a new manager is
transferred into the office, he will undoubtedly
let his attitude and philosophy be known shortly
after arriving.

Once the young broker has some indication of
the manager's style, he should keep uppermost in
his mind what every manager wants from every
broker: as much problem-free business as possible. This should be the young broker's goal as
well. The only difference between the two is that
the young broker also has psychological and
emotional needs which have to be met if he is to
reach the manager's goal.

While the broker has only one manager to get
to know and understand, the manager has to
relate to multiple personalities and needs. If he is
a good manager, he will meet at least every six
months with each of his broker's individually.
While the manager should meet this goal, the
young broker should recognize that the manager
must give first or top priority to big producers in
the same way that the broker gives top priority to
big clients. By using the semi-annual meetings,
the young broker can communicate to the manager in a professional manner what kind of support
and relationship will help him do more business.
He should start by immediately letting the manager know he is going to give the manager what he
wants, good clean business in large amounts. The
young broker sets the tone by getting this mutual
objective on the table right away, and by letting

MY WAY

the manager know he is a team player willing to do his part in helping the office achieve its goals. Invariably, the manager will respond by asking the young broker what can be done to assist him in achieving his goal. This is when the young broker can communicate his requirements, needs, and wants to the manager. These should be non-material in nature. Nothing will turn a manager off more quickly than a young broker requesting quote services, subscriptions, sales support, etc., before he has earned them through production.

The young broker should tell the manager if he needs help in a certain area. He should draw upon the manager's experience by asking questions. He should remember that the manager has as big an ego as any broker. He will help anyone who will help him achieve the office's goal. A good manager will give the pat-on-the-back and stroke when needed, but if he doesn't, the young broker can keep the communication lines open by seeking out the manager from time to time.

The young broker should only pick non-market hours to discuss his progress and ask questions. A manager is turned off by a young broker who wants to spend market hours doing anything other than prospecting or selling.

Finally, there is the situation where the manager will not have anything to do with young brokers. There is no good solution to this problem. Hopefully, there is a boardroom leader who can fill the void. In any case, the young broker should get an older broker to be a "mentor". This older broker should be one of the largest producers in the office so he can teach the younger man the right habits. Without an approachable manager, the young broker simply has to be more self-reliant. This can be positive, but it can also lead to the broker thinking about changing firms. That is always a mistake for a young broker. He has not developed a clientele which will follow him and is not experienced enough to overcome the trauma of a move. The only real solution to the dilemma is for the young broker to think of the difficult manager as just another challenge.

FWIW # 20 .... Time Wasters

In every office there are two types of time wasters. First, there are the tape watchers who spend all day in the broker's office. These individuals are fast disappearing from the scene due to the evolving layout of new offices which does not include a composite tape display. The tape watchers who are still around, however, believe they deserve a great deal of a broker's time. Since the older brokers know what time wasters these people can be, the young brokers find themselves inheriting their accounts shortly after beginning their careers.

A more serious problem for the young broker is the mediocre older broker. This is the individual who does just enough production to keep his job but not enough to be a real professional. He is usually well liked, knowledgeable, and lazy. He will spread negative thoughts and reasons for not doing business with a vigor he never shows in his pursuit of business. The danger for the young broker is that this mediocre excuse for a broker will give him all of the advice he wants whenever the young broker wants it - particularly during market hours. This friendliness is attractive to a rookie going though all the trials and tribulations

MY WAY

of getting started. The mediocre older broker holds the same attractiveness for the younger broker that a flame holds for a moth.

How should the young broker handle the situation? The obvious answer is to tell the other broker to stay away during market hours. This is hard for a young broker to do, however, because he does not want to hurt the feelings of one of the few people in the office who will give him the time of day. The next best way for the new broker to avoid wasting time is to pick up the phone when he sees the offending broker approaching. If he has already arrived and is sitting at the desk, the young broker should just pick up the phone and tell the visiting broker he has calls he has to make. Perhaps the offending broker could be asked if he has reached his goal for the day. This question will usually cause enough discomfort to send the broker packing. While most brokers won't do it, a final method of keeping the time wasters away is for the young broker to enlist the manager's help. Quietly asking him to speak to the offender will usually get the job done without anyone else knowing.

As the young broker matures, and realizes how important every minute of the day is, his concern for hurting anyone's feelings will diminish.

FWIW # 21 .... Lunch Time

Advice about lunchtime is clear cut. A broker should eat in the office or eat at the right place and with the right person. The right place is a restaurant or club where the people a broker wants as clients eat lunch. It is important to be

MY WAY

seen as well as to see. For instance, if the broker goes into a restaurant and a client or friend is having lunch with someone unknown to the broker, he should go over and speak to his client/friend. What better method is there of becoming known to someone new than to be introduced in pleasant surroundings by a mutual friend?

If there is only one major luncheon place for businessmen, the young broker should consider scheduling lunch at the same time each day and at the same table. Generous tipping will help ensure that he becomes a "regular". In a business where appearances and contacts are important, it is helpful for the young broker to have the premier restaurant host call him by name and show him to "his" table.

Under no circumstances should a broker eat lunch with another broker. That is the ultimate waste of time.

The right person is a client or prospect who is easily recognizable to others in the business community as a leader. People will stop by to speak to either the broker or his guest thereby giving the broker an opportunity to meet the right kind of prospects.

Lunchtime, if used properly, gives the broker opportunities to schedule face-to-face meetings with prospects/clients. Instead of being a time of expense, it can be very profitable.

FWIW # 22 ....Community Service

Community service for the sake of getting business will not work. The young broker should participate in a service function in order to give his community something in return for the oppor-

MY WAY

tunity to be successful. There is a very real danger, however, in the young broker spending too much time away from his business. When formulating his plans for outside activities, the broker should consider the following criteria:

(1) He should limit his community service to no more than two activities at one time.

(2) The young broker should find community services in which he can be associated with the kind of people he wants as clients.

(3) The activities should be meaningful and the young broker should get involved in such a way that he can make a difference through hard work and leadership.

(4) The broker should set goals that he can accomplish over a three year period. After he achieves one set of goals, he should rotate to other activities to widen his community awareness and broaden his reputation.

Service clubs offer the young broker an excellent way to get to know other businessmen. The problem is that he thinks the club members will make excellent prospects. Usually, it does not take long to dispel this illusion. A service club membership is a long term method of building a reputation. Only over time, after the young broker has demonstrated his leadership and professionalism will he be able to count on having some of his club members as clients.

The young broker does not have to join a service club. He could also consider working with a civic organization such as the Chamber of Commerce or a cultural organization such as the symphony, ballet, or museum. All of these areas offer opportunities for the young broker to demonstrate leadership ability as well as to associate with the kinds of people he would like to have as clients.

FWIW # 23 .... A Growth Investment?

The President of the young firm issues the following press release:

"The company has just finished a good year, and we hope the coming year will give us the opportunity to do as well. However, there is, a possibility that we will not be able to get our clients to do business again. In addition, I am not sure the economic climate will be conducive to doing business this year. Finally, our competitors are growing rapidly and they might take some of our clients because the cost of their services is less than ours."

No intelligent broker would recommend an investment in any firm headed by a President with such an attitude as described. Well, the content of that press release is approximately the same as the content of the speech most stock-brokers give to their managers each year. The young broker will fall into the same trap because he is *told* by older brokers that he has no control over his own environment. That is just not so. Just as any entrepreneur must go out and take control of his own environment, the young broker must realize that he is the only one who controls his destiny.

Any growth-oriented company faces the same barriers to success that block the broker's path. He must overcome these barriers and not rest once he has achieved a certain production level, whether it is $250,000 or $1,000,000. If he be-

MY WAY

comes complacent, it signifies the beginning of the end. He must constantly be improving his prospecting, salesmanship, and investment knowledge to be successful.

How the young broker keeps growing is the subject of the next five sections of this book. To make sure the young broker is able to enjoy a long and prosperous career, he will have to learn to stay within the CHALKLINES.

CHALKLINES

FWIW # 24 ....What are Chalklines?   *MY WAY*

Chalklines are the outer boundaries of ethical and legal conduct in the securities business. Many young brokers come to rue the days they did not pay attention in training to the material covering the rules and regulations of the securities business. Little do they know (or care) of the serious consequences they could suffer due to even accidental infractions. More importantly, young brokers do not realize how much business they will miss by not understanding the full extent of what is permissable. They are like a football team whose players know where the field is, but not where the out-of-bound markers are. The team's ability to function is so sharply reduced that before long their opponents have them stymied. Likewise, the young broker who does not know the limits of legal and ethical conduct will find himself severely restricted in his ability to do business.

The outline of compliance procedures established by his firm should be regular reading for the young broker until he understands the maze of rules which govern his business. Over one-half of the problems a broker faces each day are usually directly caused by him.

He makes a mistake or fails to catch a mistake due to his ignorance of the compliance procedures. Perhaps he opens a margin account for an employee of a bank. Perhaps he solicits the purchase of a new issue from a restricted person. Perhaps he discusses a security under SEC Registration in a letter to a client. Perhaps he fails to put an option strategy recommendation in the proper format. The infractions go on and on. The point is the broker cannot minimize his self-

MY WAY

inflicted wounds unless he knows the rules and is careful to comply with them.

FWIW # 25 ...... Be Honest with the Manager

Because of his supervisory role and the nature of their thinking about manager/broker relationships, many young brokers do not feel comfortable in having frank and open discussions with their managers when problems arise. This creates more problems. The manager must be looked upon as an individual who will protect his brokers when they make mistakes. The word protect is used in the sense that the manager will allow the young broker to explain his side of a situation and will help him bring all the relevant facts into the discussion. The broker should feel confident in the knowledge that he will not be stampeded.

It goes without saying that the best way to prevent a problem is to nip it in the bud before it comes up. A broker begins to develop a sixth sense which tells him when a prospect or client is not acting right. As soon as he has misgivings he should have enough sense to back away from the prospect/client or, at the least, to document everything that transpires between them from that time on. Going to discuss these misgivings with his manager is the smartest step the broker can take. In that way, the manager is aware of the situation and can give the young broker the benefit of his experience. In addition, if the situation does turn sour, the broker has fulfilled one of the cardinal rules of the business. By following the manager's directions, the young broker is basically freed from responsibility.

Unfortunately, the typical young broker does

not go to his manager until the problem with the client surfaces as a formal complaint. At this point, he is asked to write a "Confidential Memo to Counsel", which is a detailed narrative of what has taken place between the broker and client from the beginning of the problem. Since the memo will be given to the firm's legal department, the broker must take pains to clearly state all of the facts, including his own mistakes. Armed with this memo, the manager can proceed to minimize any damage which has been done.

A young broker's career will end if he lies to his manager or gives him only selective facts about a problem. Hell has no fury like a manager who has proceeded to communicate with a client and the firm's legal department on the basis of false or misleading information. Not only is it embarrassing, but there is the very real danger that the firm's position may be seriously undermined. If the manager has taken a stand which cannot be defended in court, the firm's lawyers must advise a quick settlement, and severe disciplinary action results for the broker.

FWIW # 26 .... Monthly Statements

One compliance requirement which not only makes sense, but, can also save the young broker a substantial amount of time while adding to his production is the regular review of clients' monthly statements. Even though it makes sense to do so, many brokers will not take the time to make this review part of their normal routine. It would seem they prefer to receive calls from unhappy clients which takes time away from prospecting and selling and the generating of income.

MY WAY

The systematic review of statements should begin the evening they are received in the branch office. Many brokers prefer to stay late at the office where they have access to the quote machine. Others take these statements home, get comfortable in a favorite chair, and go through the material in a leisurely manner. Either way, the job needs to be done as soon as possible so that the broker can spot mistakes or potential problems before the client does. The first "red flag" the broker should look for is any type of journal entry. A "JE" means someone has effected a change in the account in some way other than through placing an order. The broker should review and understand each JE since the client will assuredly ask for an explanation.

The second "red flag" is any short security position. Unless the client has deliberately sold some stock short, the short position on a statement indicates the client still owes stock on a transaction or documents necessary to make that stock negotiable. Either way, the client and broker are in danger of running afoul of the compliance regulations. Debit or credit balances at the end of the month constitute the third "red flag". Should the credit balance have been put in a money fund? Paid out by check? Is the debit balance from a duplicated check? A short dividend? Whatever the explanation, it generally means there is a potential for a problem.

Margin accounts should be reviewed even though they normally have a debit balance. Since there is more activity in a margin account, there is a greater opportunity for error.

The morning after reviewing the statements, the broker should have his sales assistant call each client with a statement problem and alert him to

MY WAY

the problem, tell him the problem is being re-searched, and give him a specific time and date when the sales assistant will call back with the resolution to the problem. By taking this simple step, the broker is able to (1) demonstrate his professionalism and concern for the client, (2) enhance the client's perception that the sales assistant is the one to speak to on administrative matters, and most importantly, (3) control his time by heading off any disruptive phone calls from upset clients during what is suppose to be productive selling time.

An additional benefit of handling monthly statements professionally is more sales and clients. This benefit comes from two sources. First, when he isn't getting disruptive calls the broker can concentrate on prospecting and sales calls. Second, the broker will generate substantial business, because as he goes through the monthly statements he will see holdings which should be switched because of changes in the markets. Clients whose accounts have been inactive are brought to his attention. The process has a rejuvenating effect on any broker's business.

In conclusion, monthly statement review not only dramatically reduces dissatisfaction on the part of clients, but also causes an increase in the broker's production.

FWIW # 27 . . . . Desk Diary

There are dozens of different kinds of desk diaries on the market. Some diaries are so detail-ed that they supply appointment spaces for every minute of the working day. Anyone who has ever tried to fully utilize such a diary knows so much

MY WAY

time is required to keep it up that there is no time left to do anything else. Therein lies the problem with trying to use a very elaborate diary. The desk diary can be a young broker's best friend if he uses it to help him instead of becoming a slave to it. Some compliance officers at brokerage firms believe every order and conversation between client/broker should be recorded. Likewise, some young brokers try to list all the prospects/clients they intend to call during the day. Both of these positions are too extreme. By trying to record every detail of the day, the broker is doomed to failure. It is not practical to record everything; therefore, the value of the desk diary will diminish because of haphazard use.

The primary purpose of the desk diary is to record appointments and their locations. The location is necessary for tax purposes. If the IRS conducts an audit, it will do so 1½ to 2 years after an event takes place, and memory will not serve well enough to satisfy the IRS. In addition, if a broker spends money for "entertainment," he must have notes on the discussions that took place which made the expense tax deductible.

The second purpose of the desk diary is to provide a record of all phone calls with compliance overtones. The broker should make a note of all calls for margin money, whether completed or not. The broker's ability to demonstrate that he actively sought a client with funds due may later be the only proof that it was the client's evasiveness which resulted in larger losses. It is necessary to record all calls for collection of money by settlement date for the same reasons. At other times, a client will call to complain about losses, or to request that money be paid or securities delivered to an individual or institution other than the one in the account title. A change of address, notification of death or divorce, and a change in financial circumstances are all examples of information which should be recorded. The outcome of a law case could turn on a broker's having kept a written record of the date he learned of events such as these.

The third purpose of the desk diary is to provide a record of "acorns" - instances where the client takes a highly risky position against the broker's advise. Unsolicited orders fall into this category as do instances where a high grade security is sold to purchase a lower grade security. Any behavorial changes in the client should also be included. Short but clear notes are all that are necessary.

Finally, the broker should make notations whenever a client gives an indication that he disputes a trade or causes the broker to "feel" something is wrong, even if he can't quite put his finger on it. The young broker should never underestimate or disregard the value of this "sixth sense" for potential problems. If there is one rule the young broker should never break, it is to follow his "gut" feelings when dealing with clients and prospects.

The type of desk diary the young broker should use is a matter of personal choice, but whatever his selection, it should have at least one full page per working day. It should remain open on his desk at all times. A closed desk diary is an unused desk diary. Finally, the broker should keep his diaries with his tax records for at least five years. The broker should obtain an inexpensive file storage box. In it he should keep not only

MY WAY

MY WAY | his desk diaries and tax records, but also his weekly or monthly production records and other important papers.

FWIW # 28 .... Fact of Life

"He is not only a good client but a good friend."

"We have been doing business together for over 15 years."

"We are such good friends, we go on vacations together."

"He is my father-in-law."

Money does strange things to people. It's a fact of life, and sooner or later the young broker will learn it, probably the hard way. Many a career has been ruined after several good years because the broker develops such great rapport with a client that they can almost communicate without words. The synergy and empathy between the two allow them to work like a well oiled machine. Then one day the broker takes a large "buy" order. The market moves against the client's position and on settlement day the client fails to pay. When the broker calls, the client refuses to pay since he distinctly remembers instructing the broker to sell and not to buy. He goes on to say that if a mistake has been made, it must have been due to the broker's writing the order incorrectly. An old fashioned "spitting" contest develops, and the broker is in for a difficult time.

Clients will try to cheat their brokers. Not just strangers, not just new clients, but old well-established clients who are fine upstanding members of the community. No matter how long an individual has been a client, the young broker should never break any rules to accommodate him. Every aspect of a broker's conduct in his business should be professional, and the broker should demonstrate by his strict adherence to standards of conduct that he expects all of his clients to be the same way.

FWIW # 29 .... "Non" Orders

"You are the expert. Do what you think is best."
"I'll leave it up to you."
"I'll be out of town, do what you think is best."
"I'll trust your judgement."
"I value your opinion. Follow it, and I'll go along with that."
What do all of these comments have in common? Every broker hears them, over and over again. They are all *non orders*. The client does not give an order to buy or to sell. The client does not indicate quantity. The client does not state a particular security. Even though the client may have only one security position in his account, he has not given an order. If the young broker executes any transaction on the strength of any of the foregoing "hints," he is at the mercy of the client. He is risking his entire career. The risk/reward relationship is completely out of kilter.

When given a *non order*, the young broker should respond as follows:
"Mr.(*Name*), I appreciate the confidence you have in me. My recommendations is to (*buy/sell*) (*quantity*) of (*stock*). With your permission I will enter an order now at (*price*). Does that meet with your approval?"

By responding to the client in this fashion, the young broker has exercised the good "judgment"

MY WAY

the client indicated he thought the broker possessed. He is also making a proposal which requires a "yes" or "no" answer. Only when the client agrees to particulars that have been spelled out is he approving direct action. Then and only then can the broker write an order and enter it in the market.

What if the client continues to be evasive, refusing to be pinned down, yet pressing the young broker to do his "best"? The broker should do nothing at all. If the client later inquires why nothing has been done, the broker can tell the client that in his best judgment, nothing should have been done. The client can hardly fault that decision after praising the broker's judgment! No matter what happens, the young broker can feel secure in the knowledge that no broker has ever been fired for *not* taking a *non order*. By doing nothing, the broker stands to lose a client, but by doing something which the client can deny he instructed him to do, the broker could lose his job. The choice is clear.

FWIW # 30 . . . . Discretion

Discretion is the execution of an order without the client's prior approval of the transaction. Discretion is legal when the client has signed a written power of attorney in favor of the broker and it has been accepted by the broker's firm. To be legitimate, the power of attorney *must* be accepted by the broker's firm. Some brokers believe they are covered when their clients sign power of attorney forms and they keep them in their desks. It cannot be over emphasized that unless the power of attorney is accepted by the broker's firm, it is not valid.

One form of illegal discretion is the taking of *non orders* covered in FWIW # 29. Even if the discussion has danced all around it, the broker is acting without the client's permission if the client has not indicated whether to buy or to sell, the quantity, the security, and the price.

A young broker will know discretion is involved if he cannot take an order, put it in writing, read it back to the client, and enter it in the market all simultaneously.

Well-meaning brokers who believe they have their clients' best interests at heart often take substantial amounts of discretion. A typical scenario features the client who indicates to his broker that he believes a certain stock will not go above a certain price, and, that it would be overpriced if it did. The client goes on vacation and, sure enough, the stock goes up until it is "overpriced." As the broker watches the price start to slip, he just *knows* the client would want the position liquidated. Looking out for the client's best interest, the broker sells the "overpriced" stock shortly before a takeover is announced and the price doubles. The broker is defenseless. His firm will pay out a great deal of money and he will be out of a job.

Finally, there is the kind of discretion which is outright dishonesty perpetrated to generate commissions. It happens because of flaws in the hiring practices as well as the pressures to produce at all costs. Dishonest or weak people succumb to the temptation of taking the "easy way out" for short term gain rather than realize the long term benefits of taking the professional approach. Supervisory systems eventually catch the broker who is dis-

MY WAY

MY WAY

honest, but usually not until he has given himself, his firm, and his profession a bad name.

FWIW # 31 .... Reading the Order Back

A young broker usually does not understand the difference between "Reading" and "Saying" until he makes an error on an order which he has to pay for. Then the difference becomes crystal clear. After he makes such an error he may pay attention for the first time to the box on the order ticket confirming that the broker has "read" the order back to the client, a box he has been checking for months.

Usually a young broker who gets a large order will feel a false sense of urgency to get the ticket in the wire room, particularly if the order deals with options or commodities. He must learn to overcome that feeling and say to the client:

"OK, (*Name*), this is what we will do. (*buy/sell*) a (*quantity*) of (*security*) at (*price*). Is that correct?" It takes less than 15 seconds to say the words that can save the problems, time, and expense of an error.

In some cases the client is responsible for the broker's sense of urgency. Sometimes the client hangs up the phone before the broker has an opportunity to read the order back to him. The broker, not wanting to offend the client, is left with an order he is not sure about. The first time it happens there is nothing the broker can do except (1) call the client back, or (2) enter the order and take the risk. The next time that client gives him an order, the broker should come out and ask the client to hang on until he has had an opportunity to read the order back. While making this request might seem difficult to some, it is not nearly as difficult as paying for an error.

FWIW # 32 ....Giving a Deposition

There are three cardinal rules to giving a deposition:
(1) Tell the truth, the whole truth and nothing but the truth.
(2) Answer questions in a short, precise manner.
(3) Have your attorney with you at all times.
Depositions are taken by lawyers when there is a dispute between a broker and a client. These disputes between brokers and clients may go through the court system or the arbitration process. Either way, the client's lawyer takes the broker's deposition, and the broker's lawyer takes the client's deposition. A deposition is the process of a witness being interviewed with the interview conducted under oath by an attorney.

Besides trying to find out the facts about the disputed matter, the client's attorney will attempt to find out anything else about the broker's temperament and ways of doing business which may be helpful to the client's case. If the broker is self-contradictory, nervous, hesitant, or evasive, the attorney will realize how this conduct will appear to a jury. One tactic commonly used by attorneys is to ask the same questions several times during the deposition in different ways to see if the witness's story will hold up. In the pressure and tension of the proceeding, this probing is not always apparent. By telling the unvarnished truth, including "I don't remember", the broker will be able to keep himself from being

MY WAY

put in a difficult position. If he later has to recap his testimony for a jury or panel, he will be able to tell the same story without hesitation.

After the deposition is over, a transcript of the proceeding is given to the broker for him to review and, if there are any errors, to correct. He then certifies that the transcript is a correct account of his testimony.

No matter how comforting the evidence is, the broker who is going through a deposition is bound to be nervous. The knowledge that what he is going to say is the truth may be the only relaxing thing about it. Whenever in doubt about the nature of a complex question or answer, he should never hesitate to consult his attorney. The broker's attorney is there to make sure the client's attorney does not take unfair advantage of the broker as well as to attempt to understand the general thrust of the opposition's case. The broker should follow his attorney's advice without question.

The compliance issue of the brokerage business can be as difficult as a broker wants to make it. The good broker learns where the CHALKLINES are, and, therefore, uses the complete playing field to his advantage. He does not have to worry about CHALKLINES, however, unless he has clients. BUILDING A BOOK, the next section deals with the difficult process of obtaining clients.

BUILDING A BOOK

MY WAY

The typical young broker has "missionary zeal." He wants to carry "the word" to all corners of his territory and convert everyone to the cause. He has faith that the solutions to all of their problems lie in the financial markets. The young broker loves to hear himself "preach." He doesn't stop to ponder the fact that missionaries do not earn lots of money, whereas successful stockbrokers do. Sooner or later, the young broker must realize that the two roles are incompatible. He cannot be a rich, successful stockbroker and a missionary, too. It is hard to imagine what makes the young broker think that his eloquent sermons can persuade a prospect who is 55 years old and has never before invested in stocks and bonds to change the habits of a lifetime. If the broker does succeed in pressuring his prospect into buying what is to him a strange and therefore suspect investment, he will regret it as soon as the market goes against his new and reluctant client. What the young broker should do instead is to find out where the prospect is in the habit of putting his money, and to offer him a similar (but superior) investment vehicle. A satisfied client gives his broker referrals when asked, while an unhappy one gives him trouble without being asked.

FWIW # 34 .... Patient/Impatient

Prospecting should be a delicately balanced combination of patience and impatience. The young broker should be impatient to get the proper number of qualified prospects into his account book. These prospects should not be mere

59

MY WAY

names that he has picked at random from the phone book, but real people with whom he has met and spoken and whom he has qualified as being worthy of his attention. He must replace his impatience for quantity with the patience that is necessary to win quality prospects as clients. He needs patience because some good accounts take years to "come around." As in any worthwhile endeavor, success comes only through hard work and perserverance.

FWIW # 35 .... From the Outside In

Every firm has a sales territory, sometimes defined by the brokerage house, but more often, by the practical question of how large a geographical area can be worked properly from a physical standpoint. Since the typical young broker begins his career with no accounts, he usually has time on his hands. As his business develops, he is able to leave the office during market hours less and less often. Unless he has an exceptionally fine registered sales assistant, the established broker does lose business whenever he is out of the office. The young broker should therefore explore his territory while he is new in the business. He should prospect, starting from the outer boundaries and working his way back toward the center. He should take the time to drive out to the most distant areas of the sales territory to pay personal calls on each prospect. During these personal visits, the young broker begins to develop personal relationships that will help him to cement business relationships throughout his entire career.

After establishing accounts in the outer areas of

the territory, the young broker slowly prospects his way back to the office. Eventually, he prospects the whole territory, develops accounts in each and every part of it, and ends up spending most of his time in the office. Any future trips away from the office should be calls on clients and prospects that directly result in order writing. In the meantime, the broker should also be developing a good working relationship with his sales assistant so that she will cover his accounts properly whenever he is gone.

MY WAY

FWIW # 36 .... Prospecting by Seminar

The seminar on financial services should be an ideal prospecting tool. In theory, it enables a stockbroker to make a presentation to a large group of investors and then to follow up on each one individually. In practice, however, attendance at seminars offered by brokerage firms is consistently terrible except in places where retirees make up a large portion of the population. The reasons for this are not readily apparent, but a careful analysis of the situation reveals both the causes of and the remedies for the problem of poor attendance.

Most of the difficulties lie in the way the typical broker goes about soliciting attendance and conducting the seminar. Even a broker who interacts masterfully with a prospect or client on a one-to-one basis may not necessarily communicate effectively when making the same presentation to a roomful of people. He tends to forget that although he calls many prospects and clients to offer recommendations, he is able to sell only a small percentage. He invites many people to

MY WAY

come to a seminar to hear essentially the same presentation only in an extended form, and is mystified when he doesn't draw a crowd.

Successful seminars begin with an interesting topic. That means a subject that is interesting to the prospect or client, not just to the broker. The subject should be one which is currently in the national spotlight. "How to..." seminars are usually well attended because people are always looking for short cuts to success. Once the broker has decided upon the topic, he must translate features into benefits in order to define the characteristics of the target audience. Only then does he determine whom to invite.

The broker should mail his invitation three weeks prior to the date of the seminar. He should mail to a group large enough to supply the number of attendees wanted. Even for a nicely packaged, well thought-out seminar on a subject of high public interest, he needs to invite at least five times as many people as he hopes will actually be there. While the number of people that *can* attend a seminar is limited only by the size of the physical facilities, a seminar conducted by one broker with the aid of his sales assistant *should* be limited to 30 or less in order to allow for the personal contact so necessary to its success.

The broker should invite only qualified prospects and clients from his active account book. Many a seminar failure can be traced to the broker's misuse of the tool. He thinks it's like a fishing net, so he casts it in unfamiliar waters, hoping to ensnare new fish. Then he wonders why he doesn't come up with anything worthwhile. The wise broker knows that the seminar is more like a rod and reel than a net. He knows exactly what kind of fish he's after, where they swim, and what they like to eat. He uses the right sort of tackle and baits his hook with the appropriate lure. He doesn't try to catch marlin in a salmon stream, or brook trout on a deep sea fishing expedition. Similarly, when a broker invites a bunch of people who may or may not have any interest in the subject matter, he gets exactly what he deserves: lots of "no shows."

Moreover, if he has not qualified his invitees, those who do attend may not have enough money to offer him any hope of new business.

In contrast, the broker who has spoken with all of his invitees and has actively been pursuing them can tailor at least part of his presentation to the known interests and investment objectives of his audience. He may obtain new prospects by encouraging each invitee to bring along a friend as his guest. Whether or not any of them bothers to do so, the very fact that the broker has mentioned it reinforces the prospect's/client's awareness of his desire for referrals.

Most prospects and clients do not perceive free seminars as being of particular value. Because they do not think of them as being worthwhile they are not highly motivated to attend them. There are several things the broker can do to enhance the invitees' perception that his seminar is important.

First, the invitaton itself should be elegant and look expensive. It should be printed or engraved on heavy, formal stock rather than typed on ordinary stationary. A format similar to that of a wedding invitation is excellent.

Second, the seminar should be held at an attractive, desirable, and accessible location - a place that people *want* to go to. The broker should arrange to hold the seminar at a country

MY WAY

MY WAY

club, restored mansion, or some other "classy" place.

Third, admittance should be by ticket only. The broker should emphasize this requirement and then adhere to it. Of course, those who make the decision to attend at the last minute should be allowed to pick up their tickets at the door. Not only does this connote an "exclusive" guest list, but the perceived necessity for permission to attend is a strong psychological factor that motivates invitees to show up.

Finally, there should be refreshments of some kind, and the invitation should advertise the fact. The simple statement: "Refreshments will be served" is sufficient. The kind of refreshments offered depends upon the location, the time of day, and the type of clientele invited. It is worth mentioning that refreshments need not be expensive or elaborate. It is better to serve good coffee and pastries or a moderately priced jug wine and peanuts than a cheap liquor and poor quality hot hors d' oeuvres. If the subject matter is timely, incorporating all of these features will increase attendance. If the subject matter is not interesting to the prospects/clients, the "frills" won't get them to come.

When it comes to ensuring a good turn-out, the young broker should leave nothing to chance. He should send out invitations three weeks in advance, and at the end of the first week he should call each invitee and construct lists of "definites" and "undecideds." If he does not have 25% more definites than he wants to actually turn out, he should send a second round of invitations. He should mail admission tickets and reminder cards one week prior to the seminar. In addition, he and his sales assistant should call each and every

person on both the "definite" and the "unde-
cided" list on the day of the seminar to reconfirm
their attendance. While these steps may seem like
"overkill," the broker must remember that for
most of his prospects/clients attending the seminar is not a high priority, and that the entire
exercise is a waste of time and money if no one
shows up.

Next, the young broker turns his attention to
questions of logistics. The seminar site and equipment must be checked and double checked. Are
there enough extension cords? Are they taped
down so that no one can trip over them? Is the
podium the right height? Does the microphone
work? Is the table for pick-up material stra-
tegically located? Are the guest register and pens
placed prominently enough that nobody can miss
them, but not so prominently that they impede
traffic flow? Is there a pencil and pad on each
chair? Is there a spare lightbulb for the projector?
Does the broker know how to change it? Is the
flip chart clean, neat, presentable, and visible
from both sides of the room? Not only must these
and other details be checked and rechecked, but
the broker should also conduct a complete dress
rehearsal, using his audiovisual aids, before the
stores close on the day of the seminar.

The young broker should rehearse his entire
presentation *out loud* at least four times before
his on-site run-through. Each time he does so, he
should actually handle his audio-visual aids and
practice his inflections and pauses for emphasis.
He should tape record his presentation, play it
back to pick out areas of weakness, make adjustments and corrections, record it again, play it
back again, and go back to work on any areas
which still need it. Nowhere is the old adage

MY WAY

65

MY WAY

"practice makes perfect" more applicable than here. Only with practice will the broker convey to his audience the impression that he is a knowledgeable professional worthy of their attention, their respect, and their business.

The young broker should start the seminar on time. If he surveys the room and, seeing that only half the people he is counting on are there, stalls for time in the hope that more people will show up, he penalizes everyone who came on time. If others do arrive late and find that they have missed nothing, they are rewarded for their tardiness, and the inconsiderate behavior is reinforced. A related point is that the young broker should give his very best performance no matter how few people are in the audience. He should infuse his presentation with the same energy, excitement, and enthusiasm he would genuinely feel if he were speaking to a "standing room only" crowd.

If the broker has done all of his advance preparation properly and is facing a room packed full of eager prospects/clients, he had better have a script that gets his audience emotionally involved with the investment ideas he is presenting and with the benefits that can be derived from implementing them. The hypothetical examples and illustrations he uses should be so clear that his listeners get a vivid and alluring mental picture of themselves as the owners of the investments in question, and as the recipients of all their benefits.

In addition, raising questions that lead into personal accounts of unfortunate experiences, specifically times of hardship and want, which the prospects/clients can avoid by doing what the young broker suggests, can be an effective technique if employed skillfully. Evangelists do it all the time, and - believe it or not- the young broker can learn a great deal that will help him in his sales presentations by watching and analyzing the pace, style, and delivery of TV evangelists, many of whom raise millions of dollars weekly.

The sales assistant should help the broker to keep track of the time without being obvious about it. The broker's presentation should last between 30 and 40 minutes and should be followed by a 20 to 30 minute question and answer period. The question and answer period should be confined to information of widespread application within the group. The broker should not fall into the trap of answering questions that are highly personal and specific in nature, or that bear no relation to the seminar topic. In every crowd, there is always one who tries to get the speaker off his subject and onto his own personal agenda. If the broker allows himself to be led astray, the good impression he has made will fade quickly.

The refreshments should be made available at the end of the question and answer period. During this time the broker and his sales assistant should mingle with as many people as possible. Both should resist the temptation to engage in serious or prolonged conversation, but should circulate, trying to either set up appointments or get permission to call the next day. Both should carry the broker's business cards, and should give them to members of the audience who are not already qualified prospects or clients.

Finally, the entire exercise is a waste of time if the broker does not follow it up with phone calls that enable him to ask for orders. The broker should contact each and every attendee within

MY WAY

MY WAY

two days of the seminar. The keys to a successful seminar, as to any part of a broker's business are: proper preparation, professional presentation, and prompt follow-up.

FWIW # 37 .... Direct Mail Prospecting

Proponents of direct mail prospecting call it "the perfect door opener;" detractors call it "the lazy man's method." Both descriptions are at least partially correct. There is a danger that a young broker may use direct mail prospecting to hide his fear of making cold calls (either in person or on the phone). Such a broker knows he must prospect somehow or other, but he is either too lazy to make cold calls or too vulnerable and insecure to handle the constant rejection that "comes with the territory." Direct mail prospecting enables him to look and feel busy, and, if he generates a large enough volume of mail, he may actually get a few new accounts. Regretably, such a broker rarely opens up enough accounts to survive in the business. The sad truth is that the broker would have been forced to overcome his reluctance to make cold calls if the option of prospecting by direct mail had not been available to him.

Although the young broker cannot depend solely on direct mail as a source of new business any more than he can rely exclusively on referrals, direct mail can be a helpful tool if it is used in conjunction with other techniques. The young broker can find a wide selection of tested and approved prospecting letters in his office. He should review all of them and pick out three or four that suit his purposes. He should mail out anywhere from 10 to 15 such letters per day, and should follow them up with phone calls two days later. The letter is a door opener in that it serves to introduce the young broker to his prospect. By providing him with name recognition, the letter may help to ease the resistance the young broker will encounter when he calls.

The thinking broker keeps track of the results he achieves with each kind of letter, gradually eliminating the less effective ones from his repertoire, and utilizing more extensively the letter that opens the most doors. He should continue to use this letter until it becomes ineffective, and should then begin the process all over again with a new group of letters.

In short, direct mail prospecting is acceptable but not highly recommended. It is very time-consuming and labor-intensive, and the young broker who is going to be successful soon finds that the most effective methods of building his book are telphoning prospects and going to see them in person.

MY WAY

FWIW # 38 .... Friends and Clients

Newly licensed insurance agents immediately go out and try to sell to all of their friends and relatives. This is exactly what the young broker should *not* do. In the securities business the maxim is: "Make friends of your clients, not clients of your friends." There is alot of good common sense underlying this axiom.

First, the typical young broker has had little or no investing experience when he starts doing business. He therefore is going to make a number of bad investments in the beginning. In addition

MY WAY

to being inexperienced, and partly because of it, the young broker is under a great deal of stress in the early days of his career. If he is doing business with his friends and relatives and making the inevitable mistakes with their money, he faces the possibility of losing his friends and losing face with his family members (or, worse, with his in-laws). The additional pressure can be enough to drive him from the business.

As time passes and the young broker's career progresses satisfactorily, his friends will ask him more and more questions about securities. At that point, since his friends have opened the door, he can respond:

> "(*Name*), I would be happy to get you some information on the subject you are interested in. Why don't we get together to discuss your investment objectives?"

In this way, the young broker puts the broker/client relationship on a professional basis from the beginning.

Finally, under no circumstances should a broker who does business with social acquaintances ever discuss their accounts with his wife. Where she is concerned, "ignorance is bliss," because sooner or later the client's wife will try to find out if she knows anything, what she knows, and how much she knows. If the broker's wife knows nothing, she has nothing to hide and no cause to worry that "something" may accidentally slip out in conversation. No matter what they say, most people do not want their friends (or their friends' wives) to know about their business. If their friends are cognizant of their financial circumstances, it is next to impossible for them to keep up any pretenses they've been maintaining, and it puts an unnecessary strain on their relationship.

The stockbroker at a cocktail party gets picked on, picked at, and picked over almost as much as the hors d'oeuvres. Some of the guests are convinced the broker is just dying to ask them about their investments so that he can solicit their business. If the broker so much as mentions the market, they scatter like minnows before a shark. Others can hardly wait to ask him about their favorite stocks so that he can tell them what wonderful securities they are and compliment the proud owners on their astuteness and cleverness. Still others are looking for free advice and "hot tips." Once they've cornered their prisoner, the interrogation begins. Yet should the broker ask a question of his own in order to formulate an intelligent answer to some of theirs, they bristle and take offense. Physicians are the prime offenders in this category. After squeezing as much information out of the broker as they possibly can, they hasten to inform him that they use a discount broker or a "professional money manager."

With a little forethought and planning, the young broker can avoid all this unpleasantness. First, he should *never* initiate a conversation about the stock market. He can rest assured that sooner or later someone else will raise the subject for him. If the person is someone the broker wants to do business with, he should listen politely. When the individual asks a question about stocks, interest rates, tax shelters, or whatever, the broker should answer it clearly, concisely, and without any elaboration. A party is not an appropriate environment for lengthy business discussions or speeches, and besides, the broker wants

MY WAY

to have a reason to call the prospect during business hours. If the broker tells him everything he knows about the subject at the party, he may bore the prospect by giving him more information than he really needs or wants, and he destroys his excuse for continuing the conversation later. If the subject is exhausted, there's nothing left to discuss. If the prospect clearly indicates an interest in having the broker call him, the broker should acknowledge his remark and set a definite time. As soon as they have finished talking, the broker should go somewhere he can be alone long enough to make notes and list everything in which the prospect expressed an interest. The next day, the broker should send him some information on those subjects. Of course, he should follow up the mailing with a phone call to answer any additional questions. Most people, unaware of the note-taking, are impressed when they receive in the mail information on topics in which they have expressed interest during a "casual" conversation. The prospect cannot fault the broker for his actions since it was he who first approached the broker. There are two possible outcomes, one good and the other not half bad. Either the inquirer will become a hot prospect and later a client, or he will never try to get something for nothing again, at least not from this broker.

If the person who starts the conversation on the market is someone the broker does not want to do business with, he can simply say:

"*(Name)*", I would rather not even think about work right now. I came here to have fun. Why don't you call me at the office and we can discuss it then?"

72

That should put a stop to the conversation about the market, but if it does not, the broker should either change the subject or turn away and talk to someone else. People do not value anything they can get "free and easy," and that includes advice and information on investing. If the broker, far from living up to the expectation that he will be "pushy," is somewhat reticent and always behaves in a professional manner, others will see him in a new and different light, and will begin to actively seek out the help they would shun if he were to offer it without first being asked.

MY WAY

FWIW # 40 .... Home Runs/Strike Outs

Young people in general, and young brokers in particular, are always looking for shortcuts to success. In the brokerage business, one of these sure-fire shortcuts is having a friend or relative who knows the manager of a large portfolio at an institution or government agency. The young broker dreams of all the commission dollars he will receive and, therefore, spends a great deal of time in pursuit of these "Home Run Hitters." This is a mistake. THERE IS NO SHORTCUT TO SUCCESS. While there is no reason not to pursue this type of prospect, the broker should limit the time spent on developing this kind of business to a small fraction of his prospecting time. Such prospects require extensive time to convert into accounts, *if* they ever become accounts, and the young broker can find himself in serious danger of losing his job because of a lack of business in the meantime. By sharply limiting the time he

MY WAY

devotes to these "Home Run Hitters," the young broker can develop his book and any success here will mean "extra" commissions upon a solid base.

FWIW # 41 .... Who? Where? How?

The unasked questions going through every trainee's mind are: Who are my prospects? Where do I find them? How do I find them? While there is an endless supply of "list" sellers, the young broker will find he has to purchase them himself if he wants one. Once he has spent hard earned dollars, he will find that most bought lists are incomplete and out of date. List buying is another of the shortcuts the young broker is tempted to take. Instead of spending money on a list, the broker would do better to invest in a map of his community, a small battery operated tape recorder, and some gasoline.

Looking at the situation logically, everyone, rich or poor, must live somewhere. It is also reasonable to assume that rich people tend to live among other rich people in nice neighborhoods or special rural areas. By driving through these areas, the young broker, using his tape recorder, can identify the streets as well as the names on mail boxes. Starting with the most exclusive areas and working down, the broker should be able to contact anyone of consequence by looking up the addresses in the cross referenced city directory to find out the names of the occupants as well as their occupations. Working one neighborhood thoroughly will enhance the young broker's opportunity for referrals.

Another method of getting names is by using the membership rosters of private clubs. While the lists are not readily available, an ingenious broker will usually find a way to secure them.

Probably the best list to use is the local Chamber of Commerce directory. This is the *only* list some brokers use. It is an excellent source.

A regional bank directory, available at the public library, will offer the young broker the names of those individuals who serve on the boards of directors of all the banks in his territory. These individuals not only have wealth, but are also considered "centers of influence" in their communities.

Using the tape recorder in his car, the young broker should take different routes to or from work. He can spot potential clients along the way. The broker should not make snap judgements about which businesses to call on. The businessman in an elaborate physical facility may not have investable capital because he has already invested his funds in his physical plant. The run down or well-worn physical facility on the other hand could mean an entrepreneur with a fat bank account and an inclination to invest. The only professional action to take is to contact each and every business along the way.

Still using the map, the young broker can canvas the individual and commercial areas block by block cold calling in person and leaving his card. Hard work? Yes, it is, but no one ever said prospecting was easy.

Last, everyone in any of the professions, including CPA's, attorneys, and physicians, is listed in the phone book.

None of these methods of prospecting is too difficult for a young broker. On the contrary, the broker can learn quite a bit about the prospect while uncovering him. For instance, suppose a

MY WAY

75

MY WAY

prospect drives a Ferrari and has his own tennis court. The broker should probably try to interest this prospect in a capital-gain potential instead of some other type of investment. "Reading" the prospect's environment can help the young broker get off on the right foot with the prospect.

FWIW # 42 ....The 300 Club

The 300 Club is not a religious organization. It should be the most exclusive private club in town owned and operated by a lone entrepreneur - the young broker. Membership qualifications should be strict. The prospective member should be wealthy, clearly on his way to being wealthy, or in control of substantial assets through his occupation. He should have a definite interest in preserving capital and maximizing returns. He should be interested in working with a professional to achieve his investment objectives. He belongs in the 300 Club. The 300 Club is the young broker's prospect list.

The club membership can number 300 or any other number as long as it is over 200 and fixed in amount. Most young brokers are told to make lists of 1000 prospects to call when they get registered. If the young broker follows these instructions he begins a method of prospecting called "shotgunning." This is the random calling of a long list of people with the aim of opening new accounts. Until he has canvassed the entire list, the young broker seldom zeros in on any one individual. In other words, only the easy accounts are opened. As is true in other areas of life, what comes easily is rarely worth having. The 300 Club is different.

The 300 Club begins, as always, with the young broker having a "suspect" list. He takes his prioritized list of questions to ask, (see FWIW # 67), and begins calling. The magic answer the broker is hoping to hear at this point is that the suspect does not have an account with the broker's firm, but does have an interest in investing. This individual becomes a member of the 300 Club. Even if the suspect indicates to the young broker that he is perfectly happy with his present broker, who happens to be his brother-in-law, the broker should still make him a member of the 300 Club. Circumstances change and the young broker wants to be available if and when they do. The process goes on until the broker obtains 300 members for the club. The number might not seem large, but it takes a great deal of effort to get and to keep 300 *qualified* prospects.

Once an individual is in the 300 Club, there are only three ways he can leave it. The first and best way is to become a client. This, of course, is the purpose of the whole system. The second way is if it becomes apparent the individual is never going to do business under any circumstnces. The broker should not consider dropping any member of the 300 Club until he has asked him for an order at least five times. The third way is if the young broker finds a new prospect who should join the 300 Club and who is better qualified to belong than the least qualified of the current members. Needless to say, the broker should attempt to make a client of his newest discovery before allowing him to join the 300 Club.

The purpose of this club is to systematize the young brokers prospecting from the beginning. Running randomly from one name to another wastes an awful lot of energy which should be

MY WAY

MY WAY

channelled productively. The benefits of forming such a club will soon be evident. Very few brokers who use the conventional approach have over 50 qualified prospects in their third year of production. If the young broker maintains the 300 Club, which requires very little time each day once the club has been chartered, he will not find his business stagnating after a few years.

FWIW # 43 ....Another's Client

Many prospects respond to a young broker's overtures by delivering one of the following classic "brush off" lines:

"I've been with my present broker for 20 years."

"My broker is my brother-in-law."

"I'm completely satisfied with my present broker."

"I'm not interested. I have a good broker."

When faced with rebuffs such as these, particularly when he's not in a good frame of mind anyway, the young broker usually takes the prospect at his word and goes on to look for another prospect. He should not give up so easily! These prospects are just the ones a broker wants for his 300 Club. These prospects may think they are happy with their present broker, but they don't know how professional the new broker is. Every young broker should conduct himself in such a way that he need not fear any other broker's competition. In order to be successful, the young broker must have self-confidence backed up by expertise and hard work.

One "come back" to remarks like the foregoing is:

"Mr. *(Name)*, I understand what you are saying. I have that kind of relationship with many of my clients. I respect your current brokerage relationships, and am not trying to interfere with them. What I am asking for is the opportunity to expose you to situations which offer you potential capital gains."

Very few individuals will turn down an offer like that. The young broker has acknowledged the present broker/client relationship, and quickly told the prospect that he is not asking him to make a choice between brokers. The implication is the prospect will have time to work with both brokers' ideas without having to make a difficult relationship change.

If he is both persistant and professional in his prospecting, odds are that the young broker will establish some sort of account with the prospect. One reason time is on the young broker's side is that eventually the other broker will put his client in a disappointing situation. Nobody in this business is clairvoyant; it happens to everyone sooner or later. If the young broker has professionally worked the prospect, he will probably get a small order at that time. Second, the established broker may retire or leave the business for some other reason. If that happens, the young broker who has patiently worked the prospect will be the most likely replacement. Third, the young broker's service and ideas may be superior to those of the established broker. If this is the case, the account will gradually be won over by his professionalism and salesmanship. The young broker who adopts a professional and persistant approach to salesmanship will capture more accounts than

MY WAY

79

MY WAY | the broker who turns away from prospects who are hard to get.

FWIW # 44 .... Marketing

When thinking about the development of business, it is the rare young broker who gives much thought to the composition of that business. The young broker who adopts a marketing approach has an opportunity to minimize some of the ups and downs inherent in the securities business. He should develop a plan to structure a clientele composed of 25% high risk takers, 35% normal equity risk takers, and 40% safety oriented fixed income clients. Prospecting can then be geared to filling a quota in each category thereby achieving the proper mix of clients. Thinking about what he is doing is all it takes to intelligently build a diversified business.

Even a specialist can build a diversified business. By varying the quality of the security and the amount of leverage used, the broker can make almost every investment strategy suitable for investors with different risk-taking profiles.

FWIW # 45 ....Consistent Service

Young brokers make a common mistake of over servicing their accounts early in their careers. Regretably, this accounts for a substantial number of lost accounts during a broker's formative years.

The young broker begins his career with very few, if any, accounts, and, therefore, finds himself prospecting all day long. When he finally

starts to open some accounts, he then has an
acceptable function to perform which he greatly
prefers to prospecting. Because servicing a client
is so much more ego rewarding than prospecting,
the young broker tends to spend more and more
time servicing the few accounts he has. Since
there are only a few accounts, he over services. As
more accounts are added and the broker continues to work the same number of hours in a week,
the level of service given each account declines.

The young broker can keep himself from over
servicing by deliberately limiting the time spent
with each account in the beginning. He can best
control the situation by keeping the 300 Club in
the same account book with his present clientele.
The broker can avoid a lopsided allocation of his
available prospecting/servicing time by spending
the same amount on each prospect and client
until he reaches the point where the size of his
"book" dictates how much time he spends with
each account.

MY WAY

FWIW # 46 .... **Time Management**

The biggest "culture shock" a young broker
experiences is the lack of control he has over his
time. In other businesses, an executive generally
can plan his day before it starts, and carry out
most, if not all, of that plan. In the brokerage
business, even the best laid plans can be destroyed by a single early morning phone call from
a client who has a problem which has to be solved
by noon. Sometimes, the broker calls a prospect
who expresses such strong and definite interests
that the broker ends up spending much more

MY WAY

time on him than he had originally intended. Once again, his plan is shot.

While the lack of control over time can never be totally overcome, it can be minimized to a certain extent. As in any business, there are times in the brokerage business when the course of events doesn't go according to plan, but such instances can become the exception rather than the rule. Part of the time control problem is a carry-over from the early days of the young broker's career, when he formed the habit of overservicing clients, and part is the result of the client's perception that a broker's time is (a) unlimited, (b) not valuable, and (c) available on demand.

The broker can set the tone of the new broker/client relationships at the time that he opens the account. After the client has made the commitment to do business with him, the broker can say:

"Mr. (*Name*), thank you for opening an account with me. Because your investments and your time are important to both of us, I want to introduce you to my sales assistant, (*Name*). (*Name*) is the administrative member of our team. She handles all calls dealing with questions about your account or statement, money fund orders, and requests for quotes. Because (*Name*) handles all of these administrative functions, I can concentrate on finding you the best vehicles for fulfilling your investment objectives. I value your time, and assure you that I will not call you unless I have information or ideas that merit your immediate attention. Likewise, if you wish to discuss a potential investment, call me at any time."

With those few sentences, the broker has: (1) taken control over the relationship between the client and himself; (2) conveyed to the client the sales assistant's duties, defined for him her responsibilities, and enhanced his perception of her role as a team member; (3) made it possible for the S/A to screen his incoming calls without offending the client; and (4) established his own calls to the client as being important and infrequent.

MY WAY

The nice thing about the entire proceeding is that the broker can use it not just when opening new accounts, but at any time. He can inform clients with pre-existing accounts of the "reassignment" of administrative functions either by phone or, preferably, by letter.

There is an additional benefit of psychological significance. By letting people know in a professional manner that he is busy, the broker not only gains control over his time, but also enhances his status in the eyes of his clients. It is human nature to perceive a busy executive as being more valuable than one who is readily accessible.

Finally, another technique of time management for the broker is not to take any incoming phone calls. In theory, this allows the broker to return calls according to his priorities rather than on the random basis in which they are received. In reality, the nature of active stock traders prevents this strategy from working perfectly. They want to speak to their broker when they call. There are two workable solutions to this problem. The first is for the broker to have a secondary phone line and give this number only to his best clients. A "private" line is also attractive to major prospects. The broker can use it

MY WAY

to advantage when selling them on himself and his firm. Moreover, when the secondary line rings, the broker will know the call is from an important client.

The second solution is for the sales assistant to quickly learn which clients are really important. A broker and sales assistant who work together as a team can stroke the clients' egos constantly. People in general, and clients in particular, cannot stand the thought that their calls (to someone they do want to talk to) are being screened (by someone they do not want to talk to). They feel even more resentful and offended if they are being blocked by a mere secretary (their perception of the sales assistant being inaccurate). For this reason, the sales assistant must never hesitate before replying to the caller's request to speak to the broker. Her immediate response should be: "I'm sorry, but Mr. (*Name*) is on the other line with a client. May I have him return your call?" When the client says yes, the sales assistant should go on to say: "I am Mr. (*Name's*) assistant. Is there anything I may do for you?"

While these methods of time management work for most people most of the time, there will always be some clients who insist upon talking only to the broker, even when the subject deals with an administrative matter that the sales assistant will eventually handle for the broker. In such cases, the broker must decide whether or not the client deserves the attention he demands. It is important for the broker to be consistent in sticking to his telephone policy. Once he has received special treatment, the client will always expect it, and if the broker does not continue to give it, he will lose the client.

MY WAY

Discounters are on the right! Discounters are on the left! Discounters appear everywhere except in the corner liquor store. To some people the question seems to be whether or not the full service broker will survive. While pressures from clients to discount are growing, ironically the greatest amount of pressure comes from so-called full service brokers who give hefty discounts rather than handle themselves in a professional manner.

To get the proper perspective on the issue, it is necessary for the broker to put himself in the client's shoes. Why does a client ask for a discount? First, like everyone, he wants the most value for the lowest cost. Second, and more important, he does not perceive any material value in the services received from the full service broker. Many clients take for granted services such as a local office, monthly statements, local cashiering, an abundant supply of research material, and a professional broker. Such clients want the best of both worlds.

A young broker is the most susceptible to external pressures to discount since he has a tremendous need to establish himself and will take almost anybody as a client under almost any circumstances. He probably is also too young to understand that he cheapens his image in his own eyes as well as in the eyes of the clients. When he agrees to discount, he confirms or reaffirms the belief that the services and advice he gives the client are only mediocre and, therefore, not worth full price.

If the broker has decided to accept some

MY WAY

discounting as inevitable, he should find out what guidelines if any, his firm has for discounting. These, of course, must form the basis for his discounting policy. Where there is no firm-wide policy, the broker should develop his own. Here is an example of a discount policy statement:

> Over a trailing 12 month period, the following discount is given on orders received in a margin account for stock held in street name. All orders should be for 1000 shares to be purchased or sold at the market.

> $ 0 to $1,000 in commissions ... No discounts
> $1,001 to $2,500 in commissions ... 10% discount
> $2,501 to $5,000 in commissions ... 15% discount
> $5,001 to $7,500 in commissions ... 20% discount
> Over $7,500 in commissions .... 25% discount

Two key elements are involved in this policy. First, the broker works out his terms in advance, so he can't be taken by surprise. Second when the client raises the subject of a discount the broker states his policy in a professional manner. There should never be any deviation from the stated policy. In this way, the broker, and not the client, controls the situation.

Should a full service broker give a discount? No. A client asks for a discount and a broker gives a discount because neither believes the broker adds any value to the transaction. The value the client is looking for is *leadership* in preserving capital and selecting potential capital gains situations. Clients drive expensive cars, belong to the best clubs, live in the most exclusive neighborhoods, go to the finest restaurants, and stay in the most luxurious hotels. They neither ask for nor expect a discount elsewhere. If clients perceive a broker to be the best and the brightest, they will use him no matter what the cost. It is up to the broker to convey that image and to deliver results accordingly.

MY WAY

FWIW # 48 .... Seeing is Believing

This kind of scenario happens all the time: A young broker cold calls a wealthy investor who agrees to a meeting. During this meeting and subsequent phone calls, the young broker gets a clear description of his prospect's investment objectives as well as precise guide lines about what the client is interested in buying. The young broker, in a burst of energy and enthusiasm, begins a diligent search for investments which fit the meticulously detailed criteria. As the days turn into weeks, and the weeks into months, the broker's feelings of self-confidence and professionalism begin to ebb, and finally turn into frustration. He does not know what he has done wrong. Every time he comes up with an investment for the prospect, the prospect turns it down. While the prospect holds out hope for the future, the only feelings the broker ends up with are frustrations and bewilderment.

What did the young broker do wrong? He made the mistake of taking his prospect at face value. It is hard for the young broker to imagine why a respected and prosperous businessman would say one thing and do another, but some of them do just that. The problem is, when some people are questioned about money matters, they give the answers they think the questioner wants to hear. Many a prospect will go on about conservative, "solid," "safe" investments and corresponding investment objectives when what he

MY WAY

really wants is a wildly speculative security which will double or triple in a matter of months. "Hot Tips" stir his blood, and despite what he says, high yielding fixed income securities with low or no rating find their way into his portfolio.

Rather than take an investor's word for what he wants, the young broker should request a list of the securities the prospect/client owns. He should then compare what is in the portfolio with what the prospect/client says he wants. More often than not, he will find some degree of difference. The broker can then vary the investments he presents to the prospect/client accordingly, thereby increasing his chances to do business.

FWIW # 49 ....Retail and Spot Secondaries

For reasons which have to do with past industry practices and the new broker's own feelings, most brokers do not participate in retail offerings or spot secondaries the way they should. If a survey of clients nationwide was taken, the overwhelming majority of people would say the broker tries to unload on his clients stocks which are "on the shelf" or "in inventory" or forced upon him by his New York office. Most brokers, particularly young brokers, share in the dislike and distrust of this type of business until the market heats up and "hot" issues come to the forefront. Even then, the unwritten rule is that a local office or broker who wants some hot issues must earn them by moving the not-so-hot issues.

Most brokers have lost sight of the fact that raising new capital for corporations is the main purpose for the existence of brokerage firms.

With this in mind, the young broker should develop a system of responding to these offerings in a professional manner. Why? First, the client gets excellent value without paying a commission. Second, the broker's firm earns a fee for bringing the investor and the business together. Finally, the part of the fee earned by the broker carries a higher payout to the broker than normal business.

When developing an approach to this type of business, the young broker will find that he generally cannot sell retail offerings successfully on a cold call. The broker needs to have done the ground work in advance. This is a good way to find interested prospects:

MY WAY

"Mr. (*Name*), from time to time my firm has the opportunity to make available either securities new to the public or large blocks of existing public securities that are owned by institutions. In both cases, we are paid a fee by the seller and, therefore, do not charge the buyer a commission. While no one should buy stock simply because there is no commission, if the stock meets your investment objectives , wouldn't you rather buy it without a commission? (Assume yes.) I would, too. Mr. (*Name*), I will clearly indentify any situation which arises and will call only if the security meets your investment objectives."

The young broker should catalog those prospects who respond positively to such a sales presentation and should call them whenever the right opportunity presents itself. Probing to find out what the prospect/client likes is the key to successfully developing this business. Calling with every offering that comes along will only get him in the habit of saying no. By approaching

MY WAY

retail issues and secondaries in a professional manner, the young broker can slowly develop this area into a significant part of his overall business.

FWIW # 50 ....Why IRA?

Mao Tse-tung once said, "A journey of a thousand miles begins with one step." So it is with IRA accounts. Every young broker goes out looking for the ideal client, who has funds to invest and who is willing to work with these funds intelligently to see them grow. Just when the broker and client begin to see the benefit of serious investing, the client calls and says he needs the money for a car, a vacation, or a new condo. Therein lies the beauty of an IRA account. When the client makes a contribution to his IRA account, he also makes a psychological commitment. The government will exact a special tax from the client if he removes the money from his account.

The second beautiful attribute of an IRA account is the constant flow of new funds each year. Not only can investments be structured to generate cash flow, but the client will add new contributions every year. Most people will go to great lengths to avoid taxes, and putting up money for retirement is about the most painless way designed to date to save taxes.

The third beautiful attribute of the IRA account is the fact it is sheltered from taxes of any kind until funds are withdrawn at retirement. This factor cuts in half the twin obstacles to accumulating wealth, taxation and inflation. Because of these beautiful attributes, the IRA ac-

90

count will become the core of every successful broker's business in a few years.

If the IRA is so great, why don't more brokers aggressively go after these accounts? One reason is that the brokerage business is designed for instant gratification. Most brokers will agree that the accounts will be valuable someday, but right now, because the client has to sign an agreement, they are too difficult to open for the small commissions they generate. This is a short-sighted view. Patience and a goal of 100 IRA accounts a year for five years will result in the broker's having huge amounts of money under his control. Through proper investing of IRA funds,the broker will find himself with a consistent source of business that is almost immune to the whims of investors.

Investment philosphy will be discussed in detail in the section on MAKING MONEY. In the meantime, a brief answer to the question of how the broker should invest $2,000: the same way he would handle $20,000, or $200,000, or $2,000,000. If he uses a money manager for large accounts, he should use mutual funds for small ones like IRA's. If the broker is going to manage the money himself, he should consider a balanced portfolio of odd lots until the account is of sufficient size to buy round lots. In other words, the IRA account should be treated as a growing entity.

FWIW # 51 .... Wrong Way Calloway

Years ago, there was a movie about a cowboy named Calloway who could not do anything right. Every young broker will come across cli-

MY WAY

MY WAY

ents who are the same way when it comes to investing. This in itself is bad enough, but to make bad matters worse, "Calloway" tends to be a genuinely nice guy who develops a strong rapport and friendship with his broker. Generally, "Calloway" takes an interest in the broker's career, gives him referrals, and, sad to report, consistently loses money. Absolutely nothing goes right for him! The broker, who feels worse about the money loss than the client does, tries harder and harder and begins to get a real complex about the situation. The broker begins to feel helpless, his stress and anxiety levels increase, and his self-confidence fades to the point that his business with other clients is affected.

What the young broker fails to realize is that there is nothing he can do about the situation. In most cases, there is no logical explanation. The poor guy is just a "Born Loser." A thorough analysis of the situation would probably reveal that "Calloway" is an investor who reacts rather than acts. He reacts so cautiously that by the time he recognizes and acts upon an investment situation, the trend has already run its course.

There are only two steps to take with a "Wrong Way Calloway" account. Since the client is usually a nice person, and perhaps a friend as well, the broker should attempt to get him to use an outside investment manager or mutual fund. If he declines to do so, the broker must emotionally detach himself from the responsibility for investment results. He should make recommendations in a multiple choice fashion so that all final decisions clearly rest with the client. If the broker still finds the emotional strain too much, he must give up the client's account since the way he feels about it has an adverse affect on the rest of his business.

FWIW # 52 .... The End

At some point in his career, the young broker will lose a good client who has meant steady, cosistent business. The episode will be devestating to the broker and his production for a time. He will search for reasons or actions which can be blamed. When no particular excuse can be found, the broker's psychological defense mechanism will create one since he cannot accept the thought that another broker proved to be better than he was.

Obviously, life goes on. The successful broker learns from this traumatic experience. He uses the occasion to assess all aspects of his business from top to bottom. What aspect of his client services is weak? In what area has the broker become less disciplined and lax? Has he started to take his clients for granted? Is he involved in too many outside activities? The list of questions can go on and on. The important point is for the broker to turn a negative into a positive. He has lost a good client—a negative. The broker's self-appraisal and subsequent corrective action will augment his professionalism—a positive.

After taking appropriate corrective action, the broker has a choice of leaving the lost client alone or going after him to attempt to win back his business. Each decision must be made based upon individual circumstances; however, if the client does not leave in anger, there is a good

MY WAY

chance the account can be reactivated. A suggested approach is as follows:

(1) *Call Client:* "Mr. *(Name),* while I realize you have moved your account elsewhere, I enjoyed the relationship we had and would like an opportunity to earn your business again. Your closing your account helped me realize my *service,* (or whatever), was not up to par. Over the next few weeks, I would like to call you with some capital gains opportunities."

(2) Handle the individual as you would an active client.

It is important for the broker to let the lost client know he would be welcomed back at any time, particularly if the broker/client relationship had been a long one. Not infrequently, a client will leave his old broker only to find he is uncomfortable with his new broker. If the old broker has left the door open and has attempted to woo the client back, a face saving situation can easily be found.

FWIW # 53 .... Account Pruning

Each year a top-quality broker should add 150 to 240 new accounts to his book. While it would be nice if all of these accounts could be the type which generates $1,000 a year in commissions, this just isn't going to happen. In many cases, these clients are people who deserve first quality service, but they just don't have enough potential for the established broker. The broker has to make a difficult decision with such accounts. He can keep the accounts and either give poor service or penalize his own earning potential. He can give the accounts to a salaried client representative, or he can use the accounts to leverage his own time by giving them to a young broker in his office in exchange for 50% of the commission for 12 months.

If the broker chooses to give his small accounts to a young broker in the office, there are some guidelines he should follow. First, the commission split should be for 50% and should last for one year. Second, all account contact should be made by the new broker without exception. Third, the receiving broker should be someone who is obviously going to succeed, and who has been in the business not less than 6 months and not more than 12 months. Finally, the office manager should be a party to the give away in order to make sure both parties completely understand the agreement. It is a good idea for the manager to draw up a memorandum of understanding and have both parties sign it.

The objective of the account giveaway is to allow the established broker to receive commissions on accounts he opened, while being able to concentrate his efforts on accounts which have the potential to produce substantial revenues. The young broker, on the other hand, is delighted to receive this smaller account, and will give it the service it deserves. Through proper service, the accounts potential will be reached, and both brokers will benefit. The office and office manager benefit because the productivity of each broker is enhanced. In addition, the client is a happy client since he works with a broker who not only pays attention to his account, but appreciates it as well.

The account giveaway program should be an

MY WAY

MY WAY

annual affair. The cleansing of the established broker's books will heighten his desire to go out and open new accounts. It will also cause him to raise his criteria for the accounts he keeps each year, and help him see the benefit of the program through an increasingly higher productivity factor as his career progresses.

FWIW # 54 ....Tough Times

Without Bear markets and economic recessions, the brokerage business would be heaven. Alas, tough times do come, and when they do, the broker learns quickly the difference between heaven and hell.

Most brokers simply stop calling their clients when the market goes down or interest rates start going up. It's as though they've gone into hibernation. They batten down the hatches and wait for the storm to abate. They even quit calling prospects! Their business declines and they begin moaning and groaning. The same professionals who know full well that stocks should be bought low and sold high become paralyzed by hysteria.

It is safe to say that today there are plenty of investments, from short-term CD's to commodities, suitable for any economic environment. The professional broker knows he must go back to basics when tough times begin. He realizes that he must do alot of hand holding with his present clients while searching out the disgruntled clients of his competitors. It is during these tough times that the truly fine professional can offer outstanding leadership to the investing public. He should take time to become knowledgeable a-bout investments the public wants at the moment as well as those which need to be purchased for long-term capital gains.

The professional broker knows that the market fluctuates constantly and will go back up sooner or later. He also knows that he must sharpen his salesmanship in order to convince his prospects and clients to position stocks or long-term bonds for future capital gains and in order to ensure that he and his clients will make money when the market moves higher.

A broker is 95% salesman. Professional SALES-MANSHIP is not a natural talent. It is a skill which must be learned like any other skill: through hard work, dedication, and practice.

MY WAY

SALESMANSHIP

FWIW # 55 ....Motivation | *MY WAY*

The best place for the young broker to look for motivation is in the mirror. The only kind of motivation that counts for him in the long run is internal. Others can help only by creating an environment supportive of his best efforts. Since there are plenty of books entirely devoted to the refining of motivational techniques, the subject is treated only superficially here. Suffice it to say that each young broker should review all the motivational materials he can get his hands on until he finds a few that really get at the heart of his own purpose in life. Once he has found them, he should read or listen to them until their content is almost second nature to him.

Some people may try to convince the young broker that he cannot and does not control his own destiny, and that external forces determine his fate. He should not allow himself to be misled. Most such arguments are nothing more than rationalizations for laziness. Once he begins to do business, he soon learns that only self-discipline can keep him moving forward on the road to production and success. As mentioned in FWIW # 6, self-discipline is not something which can be turned on and off at will. It can come only from developing the habit of doing the right things in the right way, hour after hour, day after day, week after week, month after month, and year after year. Salesmanship requires steady motivation, and motivation requires self-discipline.

FWIW # 56 ....Consistency

Just as a honey bee moves from flower to

MY WAY

flower looking for nectar, the young broker begins his career going from one approach of prospecting and doing business to another, trying many, perfecting none, and searching, always searching, for the secret to quick and easy success. The secret, of course, is that there is no secret. Consequently, the fruits of the young broker's quest for instant gratification are frustration and disappointment. What the young broker needs is a consistent approach that works for him. Even after he finds one, it will take him three to five years to firmly establish himself in his career and get on the road to a million dollar production level.

Because the young broker is not knowledgeable, he should observe, ask questions of, and *listen* to as many successful brokers as possible during his training period. In this manner, he should begin to understand their methodologies well enough to start formulating his own techniques. Once registered, he can begin to implement and refine his plans as he moves into his first year of production. It is important that he feel comfortable with his approach to selling, since selling is difficult at best and next to impossible when the salesman is nervous, uneasy, and "uptight" about what he is doing.

In formulating a consistent approach to developing his clientele, the broker should first ascertain what investment vehicle best fits his psychological profile. Since he has had little or no experience, the best way for him to do this is to research all kinds of investments while he is still in training. Once he has settled on a particular type of investment, the young broker should proceed to learn as much as he possibly can about it. He should become the resident expert in his local office. If possible, he should volunteer to be the coordinator for that investment in order to develop contacts with the experts in the firm's home office.

When the broker returns from training, he begins cold calling. While he should make all of his cold calls in the manner outlined in FWIW # 69, there comes a point where the young broker must "take the plunge" - i.e., make a presentation and ask for an order. Except in cases where it is clearly not in the client's best interest, the young broker should center all of his sales presentations around the investment vehicle he has studied in depth. There are two reasons for this.

First, the more knowledgeable he is, the more impressed the prospect/client will be with his professionalism. Second, once the client has opened an account with the young broker, his confidence in the broker's ability will spread from one investment area to others.

FWIW # 57 .... Perfectly Imperfect

It seems only sensible and reasonable to the young broker to consider as much investment information as possible before making a recommendation. He thinks that before making any decision, he should weigh all of the factors that could influence the outcome. Therein lies a major problem. The young broker operates in a world where all decisions must be made on the basis of incomplete or imperfect information. This troubles the young broker, since he tends to be a perfectionist anyway, and since he still harbors the delusion that he is going to be the first broker in history never to lose money for any of his

MY WAY

103

MY WAY

clients. This can lead to "paralysis by analysis." The broker can't do business because he is terrified of making a mistake. He becomes increasingly defensive, and invests much of his psychic energy in justifying his inactivity. He will continue to feel unprepared to make decisions until he gets over the fear that he may do something wrong. There is, of course, no way to fulfill his longing for perfect information, but there are ways he can learn to accommodate and appease it to a degree.

Since he hasn't the gift of prophecy, the young broker needs to develop a system which is the next best thing. Whenever he makes a decision on a recommendation, he should record in a notebook all of the factors he has considered. Later, when the investment has proved to be a good one or a bad one, the broker can sit down and analyze why things have turned out as they have. He can compare his findings with his initial reasons for recommending the investment. In time, his list of factors which can influence an investment grows, and so does his confidence. His "pro and con" list enables him to utilize the cumulative results of his experience in making future decisions. While the young broker will never realize his ambition to make decisions that are 100% correct 100% of the time, he will: (1) overcome his fear of operating on the basis of imperfect knowledge, (2) learn from his mistakes and therefore be less likely to make the same ones twice, and (3) find it easier to formulate recommendations/sales presentations.

FWIW # 58 .... Relationships vs. Transactions

The primary source of the retail broker's income is and always has been commission dollars generated by transactions. The more complex the investment or the harder it is to sell, the higher the commission. It is therefore understandable that young brokers think in terms of transactions rather than in terms of relationships. Only after a year or so does the average broker begin to realize how quickly a client can slip away if he sells him an investment which does not meet his investment objectives.

Throughout his career, the young broker must prospect daily and effectively if he is to resist the temptation to make a transaction which is not in the client's best interest. By carefully nurturing each client and developing a real interest in him, the young broker will help cement the broker/ client relationship in such a way that the client begins to rely on him in all financial areas. A relationship characterized by this level of trust and confidence will sustain the broker during difficult periods.

The broker lays the cornerstone for a sound relationship with his first cold call. He should show by his actions and questions that he is keenly interested in the prospect's financial well-being. He should listen carefully and make notes of the client's answers to his questions. Every time the broker makes a recommendation he should explain to the prospect/client exactly how the recommendation meets his investment objectives. They should discuss it until the client clearly understands it.

While the broker should attempt to direct a prospect's/client's questions concerning clerical or administrative problems to his sales assistant, he should make it clear to the client that he welcomes questions concerning investments, and

MY WAY

MY WAY particularly welcomes questions the client may have concerning investments recommended by another broker. The broker should also let his prospect/client know that he will keep him apprised of any significant changes in the securities markets or tax laws.

Here is a script for the early stages of prospecting:

"Mr. (*Name*), you have stated that your primary investment objective is to: (pick one)
(1) Preserve your capital
(2) Generate additional income
(3) Secure large long-term capital gains.
With that in mind, I will assist you in devising a co-ordinated, well-thought out approach to investing. Please don't hesitate to call me if you have any questions concerning an investment, even if it is offered by another broker."

As the relationship develops and the prospect becomes a client, each subsequent recommendation should contain the following statement:

"Mr. (*Name*), in the course of reviewing your investment portfolio, there is an opportunity to achieve your objectives that you should be aware of."

The broker can go on to explain any investment he has in mind.

It bears repeating that the broker should use every opportunity available to remind the client, in a subtle but unmistakable fashion, that the client's best interest comes first with him. If he begins early in the prospecting process, the young broker will find the task a great deal easier.

FWIW # 59 .... How Much is Enough?   *MY WAY*

How many phone calls per day are enough? 10? 20? 30? There are as many different answers as there are brokers. Trouble arises because the young broker is told to make 40 phone calls a day. "It's a numbers game." He begins to believe that if he dials the phone a certain number of times success will be automatic. This is nonsense, of course. What follows is a complete day of selling which will result in steady progress and a feeling of accomplishment for the young broker.

Step one is to work on the 300 Club, (FWIW # 42). The broker who is still building membership should plan to *complete* 15 cold calls each and every day. A broker who has already a-massed his 300 *qualified* prospects makes however many cold calls he finds necessary to maintain the membership level at 300.

Step two is to make eight calls to prospects/clients where a recommendation to purchase some investment is made. This number of eight is a minimum number to be achieved through *outgoing* phone calls.

Step three is to schedule five personal appointments to see prospects/clients each day. These may be initial visits (FWIW # 70) or follow-up visits involving longer presentations. Whenever possible, these visits should be scheduled for times before the market opens, after 4:00 p.m., or in the evening.

The numbers specified represent the minimum number of calls in each category. The broker should reach these goals without fail *every* day. Even if he achieves twice his quota in one or more categories on a given day, he should still

107

MY WAY

require himself to accomplish the minimum again the next day.

Most veteran brokers will question the numbers, thinking they are too low. However, if the young broker follows this system faithfully and fulfills his daily goals, even allowing for two weeks' vacation, he will make 3,600 cold calls, ask for an order at least 1,920 times, and keep 1,200 face-to-face appointments in the course of a year. The average stockbroker could consistently maintain a much higher level of productivity by sticking to this selling plan. This measured approach also ensures that the broker always has a constant supply of qualified prospects to convert into clients.

FWIW # 60 .... Prospect Storage

Every young broker has a list of wealthy people whom he just *knows* would become clients if only he would call them. This private reserve is called "Prospect Storage," and it is a pipe dream. When asked why he does not call those prospects *now*, the broker responds that he is waiting for the right investment opportunity, or for the stock market to hit bottom, or for interest rates to peak. He will wait 'till the cows come home. The truth is that "Prospect Storage" is the broker's lack of self-confidence. He does not call because he is afraid that his recommendation will be rejected, or worse, that it will be accepted only for the investment to decline in value.

To further complicate matters, the broker takes comfort in the thought that he has these "sure things" tucked away for a "rainy day." A false sense of security if there ever was one!

The young broker who is just newly licensed is
more likely to suffer from this affliction than
anyone else in the office. He goes to great lengths
to prospect with unqualified people who live out
of town or who really do not have the funds to
make purchases of any consequence. He has all
manner of excuses for this unproductive activity.
He is "testing his sales presentations." He is "just
getting his feet wet." However he puts it, it's just
another way of saying he is wasting his time.

"Prospect Storage" can be nipped in the bud by
recognizing it for what it is and by taking steps to
overcome it. As with most problems related to
salesmanship, the broker will find that belief in
his product soon translates into faith in himself.
He needs to make a concentrated effort to locate
an investment or investments that he really thinks
is terrific. It will boost his self-confidence and
enable him to make those initial calls.

MY WAY

FWIW # 61 ....Overwhelming BS

If a young broker were to record his phone
calls to his clients, he would discover two things
about them. First, they are too long. Lengthy
phone calls are time wasters. Second, he tries to
overwhelm his clients with information.

While it is important for the broker to know a
great deal about any investment he sells, it is not
important for him to pass *all* of this information
along to the client. If the broker has done his
homework and has developed an accurate profile
of the client, then he knows what will move the
client toward making a decision. The broker
should translate all pertinent information into
benefits to the client, and should feed him these

MY WAY

tidbits one at a time. He can make trial closes along the way.

There is a third reason for not overwhelming clients with information. If he oversells an investment, the client might fall so deeply in love with it that he will refuse to consider selling it when the time is right. This can be a very real problem. When an investment has proved to be very profitable for a client, he tends to want to hang onto it even after his broker has told him it's time to get out. The investment declines in value, his substantial gains diminish -- sometimes to the point where they become losses -- and he has to wait -- perhaps for a long time -- for another opportunity to make the money all over again. And whom does he blame? Himself? Nope. He blames his broker.

How long should a presentation take? As much time as necessary, and as little time as possible. In no case should it take more than three minutes to go from the initial presentation of facts and benefits to the close. After three minutes, the client's attention will begin to wander. If the client is interested enough to ask questions, the broker should answer them all as concisely as possible and ask for the order. The young broker should practice his telephone presentations until he can consistently deliver all of the relevant information in three minutes or less. While difficult to master, a brief, lucid presentation is as much the mark of the experienced professional as a long, rambling one is the sign of the novice.

FWIW # 62 .... Features vs. Benefits

Listening to a young broker sell can be an

educational experience. He rattles off a long array of statistics and information and concludes, "Isn't that great?" The poor bewildered prospect/client on the other end of the line, politely responds, "Well, I guess so. Too bad I don't have any money right now." The prospect/client is embarrassed to tell the broker that he has no idea whether the information is good or bad or, frankly, why he should give a damn about it in the first place. The young broker needs to learn that clients are busy people who require a broker to translate a multitude of complicated facts and information about a security into *benefits* they will receive by owning it. Once the broker learns this secret, his success rate in selling jumps dramatically, and, with it, his commission dollars. It is only natural for a prospect/client to want to know what benefit he will derive from following an outlined course of action, particularly spending his money. Only a fool spends his money without first getting an answer to the question, "What's in it for me?" Hopefully, the young broker will develop a clientele of smart businessmen and not fools.

Translation of facts into benefits is a little bit like learning a foreign language. To really become fluent in a foreign language, an individual must learn to think in that language. Likewise, a broker must take in facts and figures, and be able to instantly convert this raw data into benefits. Like any other skill, the ability to make these mental conversions quickly and accurately is acquired only through practice.

Translation of facts into benefits can take many forms. Some advanced practitioners simply paint a mental picture of the benefits for the prospect/client without expounding on the facts at all. This

MY WAY

111

MY WAY is acceptable, and when it's done by a professional it's beautiful to hear. In order for the broker to
pull off this type of presentation, he must first
have established a great deal of trust and rapport
with his client, and that implies a relationship of
long standing.

Another effective way of making the translation is to present both the fact and the benefit to
the prospect/client and explain to him how one
turns into the other. In other words, the broker
leads him through the process. To do so effectively, the broker must have done his homework.

In order to visualize the translation, the young
broker should take a sheet of paper, draw a line
down the middle, and label the left side FACTS
and the right side BENEFITS. Starting on the left
side, the broker should list the facts. For example,
suppose the stock in question earned money from
1973 through 1983. The broker records this accomplishment as fact # 1. Moving over to the
right side, the broker lists the corresponding
benefit. In this case, the benefit to the prospect/
client is safety since the company continued to
make money during the two worst recessions
since the Great Depression. The broker may
present this information to the client in this manner:

"Mr. *(Name)*, this company has made money
every year for the last 10 years, even though the
country has been through the two worst recessions since the Great Depression. This should be
reassuring to you since you have expressed a
concern for the safety of your investment when
purchasing stocks."

The list should include all features the broker

can think of with a corresponding benefit for
each one. A word of caution: the broker must
make sure that when he writes something in the
BENEFITS column, he is listing an advantage to
the client and not merely restating a fact about
the stock in different words. Once the list is
complete, the broker can develop his presentation from it, modifying it for each prospect/client
by selecting those features/benefits which most
appeal to him.

MY WAY

FWIW # 63 .... The Evil I

"If you could learn how to make presentations
to prospects/clients so they would be more atten-
tive and responsive, you would be interested in
learning how to do it, wouldn't you?"

Well, you just did. Most people would have
posed the same question in this manner: "I could
teach you how to make better presentations to
prospects/clients so they would be more responsive. I bet you would be interested in learning it,
wouldn't you?"

What is the difference? In the second, more
common way of speaking, "I" comes before
"you." That is also the message delivered to the
prospect/client: "I", the broker, come before
"you," the propsect/client. In selling, particularly
in dealing with an intangible such as a person's
wealth, it is important for the prospect/client to
always feel and know he comes first. In his
presentation, therefore, there is only one place
where the broker should use the pronoun "I", and
that is in the close. Only then should the broker
allow himself to lead the prospect/client. It is

MY WAY

there that he takes a stand and puts his whole reputation behind his recommendations.

"Mr. *(Name)*, I believe you should purchase 1000 shares of this security."

"Mr. *(Name)*, in my opinion, you should own $50,000 worth of these bonds."

At first the young broker will feel strange thinking and speaking in terms of "you," "your," and "yours" instead of "I," "me," "my," and "mine," but he will become comfortable with the practice as soon as he realizes that people are paying closer attention to what he says.

FWIW # 64 .... What's in a Name?

Anyone who has ever been in a crowded room or busy airport minding his own business and has suddenly heard his name called realizes how the sound of a person's own name makes him prick up his ears. It is only natural. Everyone likes to hear his name spoken. The broker needs to take advantage of this fact in selling. How often he addresses his prospect or client by name depends upon the presentation he is making, but he should say it at least three times: once during the opening, once during the body, and once during the close. A word of caution is in order here: the young broker should take care not to overdo it. If he begins every sentence by calling the prospect's/client's name, he becomes repetitious and irritating. He should address him by name only when he wants to sharpen the focus of his attention.

FWIW # 65 . . . . Practice, Practice, Practice | *MY WAY*

Everybody knows that the more a person engages in a particular activity, the better he becomes at it. Athletes realize this and daily spend hours training and preparing for competition. Yet, salesmen in general, and brokers in particular, are horrified if someone suggests that they should write out their presentations beforehand. "But", they protest, "I don't want to sound 'canned'," or "A canned speech would lose me the sale." Apparently they think there is some sort of mysterious degradation associated with logically working out a presentation and having it prepared and practiced beforehand! The same salesmen who hold these beliefs will spend hours hitting golf or tennis balls in order to be better at these sports. Is it less important to be professional at the office than at play?

By taking the time to fit the pieces of a sales presentation together in a logical and persuasive manner, the young broker not only helps himself, but he also helps his prospect/client. By helping him really comprehend the opportunity being presented, he increases the chances that the client will take advantage of it. If the prospect/client fails to appreciate the nature and potential reward of the investment, he certainly isn't going to buy it.

FWIW # 66 . . . . Listening

People like to hear themselves talk. Salesmen are not exceptional in this respect. The problem with that is the salesman needs to ascertain his prospect's/client's wants and needs in order to

MY WAY

effectively perform the sales function. If the salesman is always doing the talking, he can't find out what the prospect/client wants. And since people *enjoy* hearing themselves talk, and it is desirable to get the prospect/client in a good mood, the salesman should allow his prospect/client to talk more.

The way for the young broker to get prospects/clients to talk more is for him to ask open-ended questions and then shut up. When the prospect/client starts talking, the broker should gently guide him through a financial inventory of assets, liabilities, and, more importantly, expectations, wants, and needs. By listening to what the prospect/client says, the broker can begin to get a mental picture of what he can do to meet the prospect's/client's investment objectives.

FWIW # 67 ....Questioning

One sales technique which the young broker must utilize from the beginning is that of asking effective questions. To obtain pertinent information and *meet minimum goals* with each phone call, the broker must guide the client along a path of increasing openness. Since few people want to give without receiving anything in return, an effective method of building communications is for the broker to share information about himself in return for the information from the prospect/client.

"Mr. *(Name)*, do you have any children or grandchildren?" This is generally considered a non-threatening question since most people enjoy talking about their children or grandchildren. Once he receives an answer, the broker can respond with a sharing comment as well as another question.

"You are most fortunate. I have ____ number of children. Their ages are ____ and ____. How old are your children (grandchildren)?"

In this case, the broker is tactfully leading up to asking what provisions have been made for their college education. The broker then works his way around to making an appropriate investment recommendation to take care of a financial need that worries most parents.

Another excellent questioning technique a broker can use, particularly with reticent prospects/clients, is to offer multiple choice answers along with the question.

"Mr. *(Name)*, when you retire, what level of income do you feel you will need to maintain your lifestyle? $50,000? $100,000?"

This prompts the individual to formulate a response. The young broker should take the time to develop questions which help him seek out pertinent information. He should take a pad of paper, set up a sheet for each of the major investment objectives, and list as many different kinds of questions as he can think of which might elicit the desired information from a prospect/client. Another approach to the exercise is to begin by listing the types of prospects he will be talking to. The main point is the young broker needs to prepare his line of questioning and the sequence of those questions in advance of his conversation with a prospect/client.

FWIW # 68 .... Dial-A-Goal

Assume for a minute a young broker has deter-

MY WAY

117

MY WAY

mined that Bob Wilson is a viable suspect to become a prospect because he lives in a large, restored, English Tudor house with a three car garage on Elm Street, the best address in town. The broker has recorded Bob Wilson's name on a prospect card and looked up his phone number and begins to reach for the phone. Is he going to have a successful prospecting call? Probably not, because the young broker has given no thought to what he hopes to achieve by the prospecting call except that perhaps he may sell some investment or that Bob Wilson may allow him to call again in the future. This lack of preparation is why young brokers go through such frustrating and fruitless times when prospecting.

The young broker should pre-plan every contact with a prospect/client and should establish a minimum goal for each contact. The maximum goal is, of course, to get an order. Since the broker will not get an order every time he makes a call, he should establish alternative goals. Taken together these goals should form a chain of information which gives the broker an increasingly clearer indication of what the prospect/client wants or needs in the way of investments. The broker should have the record of past information collected in front of him when he makes the call. He should not touch the phone until he has reviewed this information and has written out his minimum goals for the call along with the questions he plans to ask. With these written goals and questions in front of him, there is less likelihood that he will forget the purpose of the call or the questions he needs to ask in order to achieve it. All of this may seem like an awful lot of work, but it is a far more productive use of time for the broker to prepare before phoning than to make 20 calls but make no progress toward securing an account or order.

FWIW # 69 .... **The Cold Call**

An established broker watching a young broker make cold calls doesn't know whether to laugh or to cry. The young broker either tries to entrap the suspect into agreeing to be solicited in the future, or assumes the role of a college professor and attempts to impart to the poor soul on the other end of the line everything he learned while in training. Both of these approaches is as much a waste of valuable time and energy as the missionary approach. (FWIW # 33).

There are no perfect approaches to cold calling, but the following suggested format avoids the pitfalls most often encountered. It should be clearly understood that this script is not designed to elicit an order. While it is professionally acceptable in some places to ask for an order immediately, in most cases it is also fruitless.

The maximum goal of this initial cold call is to get an appointment to see the prospect, *if, after talking to him, the broker wants an appointment.* The minimum goal is to find out if the suspect is worth pursuing.

"Good morning, Mr. (*Name*), this is Dan Jones at XYZ Brokerage Firm. Do you have an account with XYZ?"

This should be the first question because many a new broker has spent countless hours and energies wooing prospects only to find they already have active accounts at his firm. If the answer is "Yes", the second question should be,

"Who is your broker?"

MY WAY

Interestingly, a client does not always know what firm his broker works for. The suspect might do business with a broker at another firm, but think it is the only one in town. Assuming the suspect gives the name of a broker at XYZ, the response should be,

"He/She is an excellent broker, I'll tell (*Name*) I called in error. Have a nice day!"

Every actively prospecting broker is going to run across clients of other brokers in his office. If he handles the situation as suggested, there can be no legitimate complaint from them.

If, the suspect's answer is "No", that he does not have an account at the young broker's firm, the next question should be,

"Do you invest with any other brokerage firm?"

If the answer is "No", the broker should realize this suspect does not qualify as a prospect for stocks and bonds. The broker should shift to another line of questioning.

"Are you aware, Mr. (*Name*), that XYZ has 6 mos., 2½ yr., 5 yr., etc. CD's; money market funds; and tax shelter IRA's? Do you presently have any CD's?"

The quality of the list of names used will determine how often the broker will have to take this line of questioning. Most wealthy individuals do some business with a broker.

If the suspect says "Yes" to the question of using another broker, he becomes a top priority prospect and joins the 300 Club. Even if the prospect states that he is perfectly happy with his present broker, who happens to be his brother-in-

law, he still becomes a top prospect. The next
question should be,

"May I ask what firm you use?"

It is important for the broker to know what
firm he is competing against. By having this
information, he can better guage the quality of his
competition and can be aware of the types of
investment services available. If the prospect declines to give the information, which is highly
unusual, the young broker should not press but go
directly to asking for an appointment. If the
prospect does indicate the name of the firm, the
broker should ask,

"Mr. (*Name*),what is it you like the most about
your present broker?"

The directness of the reply will give the broker
an indication of just how strong the relationship is
between the prospect and his present broker. The
young broker should acknowledge the answer
and go on to say,

"That is interesting. My function is to assist my
clients in finding the right investments. While I
recognize your present relationship, I would like
an opportunity to meet you. My visit will take no
longer than five minutes, and I will not try to sell
you anything. When would be a good time for us
to meet?"

The prospect will undoubtedly try to put the
young broker off with a response such as:

(a) "I'm perfectly satisfied with my present
broker," or
(b) "I don't have time to see you."

The broker should respond with the following:

MY WAY

121

MY WAY

"Mr. (*Name*), (a) I'm sure you are happy with your present broker, or (b) I know that you are a busy man. I want to emphasize I am not going to try to sell you anything. I would like to meet you in person. I am only asking for five minutes of your time, at your convenience, so we can get to know each other better. What would be a convenient time?"

After the second attempt, most prospects will agree to a visit. Those who will not can be recycled for a call back in a few weeks. In either case, the broker should end the call by saying,

"Before I hang up, would you like some quotes on stocks you own or have an interest in?"

If the prospect answers "Yes" the broker should ask,

"Do you own some? How many shares?"

The broker should conclude by saying,

"Thank you for your time."

"I look forward to meeting with you. Have a nice day!"

In reality, cold calls do not always go according to the script. However, the cold call format that has been outlined reduces the inefficiencies in prospecting, and helps the young broker establish who is and who isn't worth pursuing.

FWIW # 70 .... **Initial Meeting**

Once the young broker has secured the initial meeting with the prospect, he should focus on the two objectives that he is supposed to accomplish. The first is to gather information about the prospect which will enable him to devise an investment strategy appropriate for the prospect. The second is to begin developing some sort of a relationship with the prospect. Assuming that the initial meeting is the result of a cold call, the prospect probably does not know the young broker on sight. If, however, the broker is going to the right places for lunch, is a member of or a frequent guest at the country club, is involved in civic affairs, and attends cultural events, there is a good chance that the prospect will have seen his face and that he will at least "look familiar" to the prospect. That kind of recognition combined with subsequent contact will reduce the sales resistance the broker normally encounters.

One advantage of going to see the prospect in his own "natural habitat" is that the broker can gain insights into the prospect's personality. For example, if the broker enters the prospect's expensively furnished office and sees an entire wall covered with awards, trophies, plaques and certificates commemorating his accomplishments, the broker had better address himself to stroking the prospect's sizeable ego. He should structure his approach differently than he would for the widow whose modest but homey living room is overflowing with pictures of her grandchildren and whose late husband handled all the family finances.

The young broker should set minimum and maximum information gleaning goals and should formulate specific questions prior to the meeting. In addition, if he has arranged the meeting with the promise that it will not last more than five minutes, the broker must get the prospect to do

MY WAY

123

MY WAY

most of the talking in order to come away from the meeting with the answers he was seeking. The broker should get right to the point and should encourage the prospect to give pertinent information while discouraging him from rambling into irrelevant areas. As a rule, most prospects really do not care whether the meeting takes five minutes or ten. However, since the broker has made a point of taking only five minutes, he may want to remove his watch and place it in front of him to keep track of the time. Not only is this good salesmanship, but it also has a psychological effect on the prospect conducive to rapid-fire questioning and staying on the subject at hand. If the broker is doing his job well, he can almost count on the prospect's asking him to carry on after the five minutes have elapsed. The broker opens the meeting:

"Mr. *(Name)*, thank you for giving me the opportunity to meet you. (Comment on attractiveness of surroundings if appropriate.) As I mentioned on the phone, the purpose of this meeting is for you to have an opportunity to make contact with an excellent firm which offers people like yourself income and capital gain ideas. Recognizing that your present brokerage relationships are satisfactory to you (if he has said they are), it would be most helpful to know..."
Here the broker goes in to the line of questioning he has developed to control the prospect's responses and fulfill his goals for the meeting.

After four minutes and thirty seconds of the meeting, the broker should "test the water" to see if he needs to wrap up or if the meeting is going to continue. Here is a good way for him to handle this:

"Mr. *(Name)*, our five minutes are about up,

124

and it is important that you understand my function is to assist clients in investing their capital in such a way as to preserve what they have as well as providing the opportunity for capital gains. You have given me some information which helps me to recognize the kinds of investments that would assist you in meeting your goals. Is there a particular investment criterion which is especially important to you?"

The prospect's response tells the broker whether or not the meeting will continue. A "no" or a short answer basically concludes the interview, while more lengthy remarks signal the broker to go on trying to elicit information.

As the broker prepares to leave, he closes like this:

"Mr. *(Name)*, it has been a pleasure meeting you. Thank you for your time. There is one point which should be mentioned. My clients enjoy the fact that they do not get interrupted by unnecessary phone calls. Please don't think I have forgotten about you if you don't hear from me for awhile. When I do contact you, you will know the call is important and in your best interest."

A final point about the initial meeting: the broker should arrive early enough to spend a little time talking to the prospect's secretary about her investments. Generally, this is best accomplished by discussing an IRA account. Thus, the broker not only doubles his chances for opening an account, but he also softens up a potential barrier to speaking with his main prospect when he calls in the future.

FWIW # 71 .... **Selling the Sizzle**

"Sell the sizzle and not the steak" is an old

MY WAY

MY WAY

adage in the selling profession. It's another way of saying sell benefits and not features. Easier said than done. (See FWIW # 62)

The call recommending the prospect/client take some investment action must be structured in such a way that it gets right to the point but not before addressing the benefits to be received by taking action. The following is an outline of a sales call which should last no more than three minutes and end with the broker asking for the order and a referral.

(1) Introduce self and identify firm.
(2) Give reason for the call.
(3) Question client's interest and time availability.
(4) Make presentation.
(5) Ask for order and referral.

Each part is crucial to a smooth presentation. First, it is common courtesy for a caller to start by saying who he is.

"Mr. *(Name)*, this is Bob Wilson at XYZ Brokerage Firm."

Clear, friendly, and professional. If the young broker has been prospecting by asking questions and building a picture of prospect's/client's objectives from his answers, he should have an understanding of those objectives by now. The young broker uses that understanding to identify the rationale for the call.

"You have indicated you wanted to find an investment which would help you to accumulate funds sufficient to pay for your daughter's college education. Do you have a couple of minutes to hear about one such investment?"

The broker has stated the rationale for the call and asked for the prospect's/client's undivided attention. The typical young broker fails to ask for the prospect's/client's attention or, in some cases, don't seem to care about getting it. Perhaps this is why the young broker's closing percentage is so low. The prospect/client may be in the middle of an important conference. He may have had an argument with his boss or his wife. Any number of things may contribute to an unreceptive mood. If the client is in a totally negative frame of mind, the broker should not waste his time and effort. To continue can only be counterproductive. If the broker receives any answer *less* affirmative than "Yes", he should respond:

"Perhaps it would be better if I called back at another time. When would be the best time for you? After 5:00 p.m. today? Tomorrow morning?"

Under no circumstances should a broker start the presentation without the prospect's/client's complete and undivided attention.

The presentation itself should be a clear and logical explanation of the benefits the client will receive from making the investment. This part of the call should be no more than two minutes in length and should conclude with a question:

"Mr. (*Name*), do you see the opportunity this investment affords you to fully fund your daughter's college education?"

If the prospect/client responds "No", then the broker should ask:

"What don't you understand?"

The broker can deal with the prospect's/client's objections by showing offsetting benefits in the transaction.

Once the question and answer session is over, the broker should close the conversation in an aggressive and forceful manner. The pronoun "I" should now be introduced into the presentation.

MY WAY

127

MY WAY

"Mr. (*Name*), I recommend that you purchase (appropriate amount) of (name of security) so that you can take care of your daughter's education."

If the answer is "No", the broker should ask why not and start asking probing questions again. If "Yes", this response is appropriate:

"You have made a wise decision. I will enter your order to purchase (appropriate amount) of (name of security) now. Do you know someone else who would like to take care of their children's (grandchildren's) college education now?"

The broker should thank the prospect/client for the referral if he gives one and should terminate the call. While this method of making recommendations takes prior preparation, the young broker will find it worth his while to use it.

FWIW # 72 ....The Right Bait

Even if a broker prepares properly and takes every step of the prospecting process correctly, there are times when he just cannot get the prospect to commit to anything. The prospect is polite, willing to listen, accepts the merits of the investment, yet will not buy. When this situation develops, there is one line of last resort for the young broker. He should appeal to the greed which is in everyone to some extent. He makes this appeal by means of a highly speculative, low priced stock which stands a chance, however slim, of going up in the *long-term*. It should be clearly understood that the broker should not resort to this tactic under normal circumstances. The recommendation is a last ditch effort before giving up on a prospect.

The recommendation should be for a minimum of $10,000 or 5,000 shares, whichever is greater. The broker's presentation should be factual. It's sole appeal is to the emotion of greed. The broker should not attempt to make it something else. As a part of the presentation, the broker should tell the client the certificate will be registered and shipped to him for him to put in his safe-deposit box. Under no circumstances should the stock be kept in the account, since that would remind the client of the lack of price movement month after month.

Generally, after the client has committed to a transaction of any kind, even one such as this, he will be more receptive to future calls from "his" broker. That is the sole reason for using this tactic.

FWIW # 73 .... **Build on Success**

A great number of broker/client relationships begin slowly with small amounts of capital while rapport develops between the two parties. The young broker can shorten the time span it norm-ally takes to build this rapport by taking advan-tage of successful recommendations he has made in the past. For example, perhaps a young broker positioned 1,000 shares of 123 Corp. stock in a client's account six months ago. Since the stock has appreciated in value somewhat, the broker, who has another excellent recommendation, would mention the 123 stock in his presentation:

"Mr. (*Name*), this is Bob Wilson at XYZ Broker-age Firm. Six months ago you made a decision to purchase 1,000 shares of 123 Corp. and the stock has appreciated nicely. Do you have a couple of

MY WAY

minutes to hear about a situation which looks as good as that one did? (Assume yes) The presentation should continue in a normal fashion:

"Mr. (*Name*), you should not disturb your present position of 123 Corp.; however, I recommend you purchase 1,000 shares of 345 Corp. to meet your objective of long-term capital gains. Shall I enter your order?"

If the client says "Yes", the rest of the presentation and request for a referral goes the same way as it did in FWIW #71.

There is no question that success breeds success. As a professional, the young broker must aggressively use his successes to get more assets under his control. Prospecting becomes a great deal easier when the broker helps the client to identify and remember successful investments.

FWIW # 74 .... Ask and Ye Shall Receive

One of the secrets of success in sales is to ask for the order - with conviction. As stated earlier, (FWIW #63), the broker should place himself unequivocally behind each recommendation he makes. The only question at this point is the size of the order. Because it is customary to ask for numbers of shares in multiples of 100, the young broker rarely gives any thought to the impact of the investment on the overall portfolio. The broker should determine the optimal investment unit for the portfolio in question. The size and number of investment units depend upon the client's (1) portfolio size, (2) risk taking ability, and (3) the broker's or money manager's investment philosophy. Some brokers believe a portfolio should only contain five stocks at one time and others believe a portfolio should be diversified with twenty issues or more.

The broker must understand the rationale behind the investment unit concept if he is to be able to convince his client of its merits. If a client purchases 200 shares of a $20.00 stock and 200 shares of a $50.00 stock, his total investment is $14,000. If the $50.00 stock retains the same price and the $20.00 stock moves on to $30.00, a 50% gain, the overall value change in the portfolio is from $14,000 to $16,000. The total return is 14%. If the broker had used the investment unit concept and put one half of the funds in each stock, the client would have owned 350 shares of the $20.00 stock and 140 shares of the $50.00 stock. With the same price movement, the value of the portfolio would increase to $17,500, for a total return of 25%. By giving each investment decision the same weight, the broker insures that his successful decisions will have an impact on the portfolio.

Even though the investment unit concept has been used by portfolio managers for years, it is a relatively new concept for brokers and their clients. By explaining the logic behind the concept to his client, the broker can enhance his professional image. Both parties will feel more comfortable in purchasing increasingly larger amounts of securities as the portfolio grows.

FWIW # 75 .... Referrals

Every young broker knows that the two most important requests a salesman can make are: "Asking for the order and asking for the referral." Yet, when a broker makes a presentation he rarely asks for a referral. Why not? Probably

MY WAY

because he's embarrassed or too proud. Perhaps he thinks asking for help is "stooping" or he's afraid he will give the impression of being "pushy". However he rationalizes it, it is actually a lack of self-confidence in his abilities or his recommendations that keeps him from asking for referrals. As in every other aspect of his selling, there is a professional way for him to ask for referrals and to build the flow of referrals into his normal everyday relationships with his clients.

The first request for a referral should be included in the first presentation a young broker makes to a new prospect/client. When he opens an account, the broker should send his new client a welcome letter which incorporates a request for referrals as well as an explaination of how to do business with the firm. The letter should go something like this:

Dear Mr. *(Name)* :

Thank you for opening an account with us. The word "us" is used since you have actually hired a team of three. The first part of the team is XYZ Brokerage Firm, which is dedicated to bringing you quality executions and research.

The second team member is Ms. *(Name)* , my sales assistant. Her function is that of an administrative manager. She has responsibility for seeing that all aspects of your account are handled properly. In addition, she will handle all money fund purchases and sales. Please do not hesitate to call her with any questions of an administrative nature.

My function is to search out and present to you investments which meet your investment objectives. By concentrating my efforts on your investments, I can help you preserve your capital and add to it as time goes by.

Finally, Mr. (*Name*) , since you have placed your confidence in our investment team. we ask you to assist us in finding other successful individuals, who need the services of an investment professional. Please take a minute to jot their names and addresses on the enclosed card and return it in the self-addressed envelope.

Thank you again for the confidence you have placed in our abilities. We look forward to a prosperous relationship.

Sincerely,

MY WAY

While the letter obviously serves many other purposes, it also establishes in a professional manner the desire for referrals. By making certain every presentation ENDS in a request for a referral, the young broker will quickly form one of the habits necessary to his success.

Needless to say, when a referral is given, the broker should handle it promptly and professionally. No matter what the outcome, the referring client should immediately be apprised that contact has been made. This feedback is gratifying to the referring client and will motivate him to make additional referrals.

A final method of asking for a referral should take place on the anniversary of a client opening an account. The broker should design a short, no more than six questions, questionaire, which enables the client to update his investment objectives as well as to rate the service he has received. The last question should be a request for the names and addresses of three business associates or friends who have a need for professional brokerage services. Very few brokers use this approach to prospecting, so the broker who does

MY WAY

so should find that it has a positive effect on the growth of his clientele.

FWIW # 76 ....Mission Accomplished

When he has received the order, asked for the referral, and thanked the client in a professional manner, the broker should HANG UP -- and go on to the next item on his agenda.

FWIW # 77 .... The Ideal

If a young broker is going to prospect, he should concentrate on wealthy people who are serious about preserving the capital they have as well as taking calculated risks with the intention of increasing their capital through long-term capital gains. This does not mean that he should turn away all other kinds of business. It does mean that a young broker should set a minimum goal of opening two of these "guided" accounts per month throughout his career. Ideally, he would have nothing but this type of account. Now, there is something worth striving for!

A closer look at such accounts reveals that they are committed to the stock and bond markets, use margin accounts, and have as their primary goal long-term capital gains. Such an account has a minimum equity of $25,000 to start. While the account is non-discretionary in nature, the broker expects the client to follow his recommendations. The responsibility for performance clearly rests with the broker. The client, in addition to following the broker's recommendations, looks upon this account as long-term capital which is not to be utilized elsewhere.

Very few brokers make a conscious effort to open these accounts because of the heavy responsibility they entail. This is not to say that few brokers trade or speculate, but that very few brokers do it in a professional manner. A major factor in unprofessional trading and speculating is the injection of the client's opinion into the decision-making process. The average client has not been trained to make intelligent investment decisions. However, very few clients are willing to admit this, so the broker must prospect diligently in order to find those who are.

Ideally, the client segregates the funds allocated to this "guided" account so the income generated can be reinvested and not spent. The account is handled in the same fashion as one managed by an investment counselor. Before beginning to do business, the broker and client agree to written investment objectives, periodic face-to-face reviews of the account, and annual measurement of results against clearly defined averages or goals.

The presentation for this "guided" account is longer than a presentation recommending a purchase of some security, but it still should take four minutes or less to present. A suggested script is as follows:

"Mr. *(Name)*, many times in the past you have expressed the desire to achieve significant long-term capital gains. Is that still one of your goals? (Assume "yes") Do you have a couple of minutes to hear about a way of achieving that goal?"

"Because you are a businessman (professional, etc.) who excels at his chosen profession, it is difficult for you to spend the time needed to

MY WAY

135

MY WAY

successfully invest for long-term capital gains. That leaves you with two choices if you want to achieve your goal. The first choice is to purchase a mutual fund. Beyond picking the fund itself, you have no control over what is bought and sold (for you)."

"The second choice, Mr. *(Name)*, is to open what is called a "guided" account. Such an account has a minimum equity of $25,000 and is set up to use other people's money when the cost of borrowing money is less than the return available to you. The objective of the account is long-term capital gains and the accumulation of money."

"As in any business operation, you, as the owner and CEO, would hire professional management. In this case, as your account executive, I would be employed to handle the day-to-day management of the portfolio. You would make all the decisions based on my recommendations. While you would have the right to veto any recommendations I made, it would be expected that normally you would follow my advice."

"Since there would be no contract, you could fire me whenever you wanted. However, normal business sense dictates that you give this new "business" at least one year to show results. You could monitor your progress through the regular monthly statements as well as quarterly reviews."

"What I am proposing, Mr. *(Name)*, is the introduction of professional investment management to your stated objective of accumulating wealth. The "guided account" will give you the discipline you need to accomplish your goal. When would you like to get started?"

Since this type of account is obviously not suitable for everyone, the broker must make sure he prospects sufficiently in order to meet his goal of two guided accounts per month.

The broker puts his reputation and career on the line when he goes after this type of business. There is no excuse for failure. The broker accepts total responsibility from the beginning and had better be able to succeed. Succeeding means MAKING MONEY, and that is the subject of the next section.

MY WAY

MAKING MONEY

FWIW # 78 ....Why Stocks and Bonds?   *MY WAY*

The 1970's and part of the 1980's have apparently been tough times for stocks and bonds. It has been argued that real estate is the only investment which goes up. This thinking is inaccurate, of course, as anyone who actively invests in all investments knows. There are several reasons why stocks and bonds are *superior* to real estate as investments.

First, stocks and bonds offer the investor far greater liquidity than real estate or other "tangible" investments. Securities, the collective term for stocks and bonds, can become collateral for borrowing if they are deposited in a brokerage account. During market hours, a client can obtain a price quote and sell his securities the same day, and have cash in hand within five business days. There is no such national market mechanism for real estate. The process of selling real estate, even at "fire sale" prices, is cumbersome and time consuming, and the cost is high.

Second, the value of real estate goes up because of (1) population growth in an area, and (2) the declining value of the dollar or inflation. Securities can go up in value for the same reasons, but also because the businesses the securities represent create wealth that reaches beyond a single community.

Third, bonds offer an income stream, within the limits of solvency of the underlying business or government, as well as a fixed term when the principal amount of money will be returned. In times of high inflation, these characteristics are seen as being negative; during periods of low inflation or deflation, however, they would become positive. While most economists and invest-

MY WAY

ors today do not believe deflation is possible, history indicates that both inflationary periods and deflationary periods are inevitable. Stocks do not offer fixed yields or maturity dates, but they do offer the potential for ever increasing yields and the ability to grow in value as the business grows.

Fourth, securities are portable. Few people are aware that this is an advantage. Ours is a mobile society. When an american's wealth is in the form of securities, he does not have to worry about leaving significant assets behind when he moves.

Fifth, the tax structure of state and local governments is based upon some form of ad valorem tax on real estate. At the same time, the taxes levied on intangible assets, such as securities, are very low or non-existent. As governments search for more revenues, it is possible the gap between the cost of real estate and the cost of securities may widen still further.

Sixth, the cost of carrying real estate assets is substantially higher than intangible assets such as securities. Real estate needs regular maintenance. The costs of upkeep add up to significant amounts of money over time. In addition, it is necessary for the real estate owner to hold liability and property insurance. As with the cost of maintenance, the cost of insurance coverage mounts up over time. In contrast, the cost of a safe-deposit box or brokerage account with a financial institution is all that is required to maintain and insure the safety of securities.

Finally, the cost of buying and selling securities is less than the cost of buying and selling real estate. Even though a real estate commission is customarily paid only by the seller, this commission usually runs from 7% to 10% of the sales price. In securities, a commission or mark-up is generally paid on both the buy side and the sell side. This commission/mark-up usually amounts to a mere 2% on each side of the trade if the total value of the transaction is significant.

While there are seven reasons why securities are at least equal to, if not superior to, an investment alternative in real estate, the only reason one investment should be chosen over another is because it comes closer to meeting a client's investment objective. There is *NO* one "magic" decision. A professional broker must be able to intelligently discuss and review all types of investments.

MY WAY

FWIW # 79 .... Scientific Art

Americans like to have precise, scientific answers to their questions. This is one reason the computer has made such great strides in the trading area of Wall Street during the last fifteen years. Institutional investors use the computer not only to attempt to predict the future of the economy, but also to try to determine which security has the lowest perceived risk with the highest perceived reward. Nowadays, studying journals which deal with investing requires advanced knowledge of mathematics and quantitative analysis as well as investments. All of this tends to give the public false impressions that successful investment decisions can be made with a degree of certainty.

There is no question that computers and mathematical models can assist in the decision-making process, principally by allowing the decision

MY WAY

maker to review several alternative scenarios. While a computer can cut time-consuming number crunching, it cannot make judgements as to what to do with the data. If anyone had infallible decision-making power, the investment game would be over, and all of the money would belong to that decision-maker.

Scientific principles can be integrated into certain elements of investing, but investing wisely and well will remain an art. As valuable as the computer is, the human ability to step outside the emotions of the moment and question the real value will always be needed in the investment process. The student of human behavior can predict future trends which the statistician/analyst can identify only after they are well established. Likewise, perceptive reasoning is necessary to realize the end of a trend before it comes.

To many in the brokerage business, a gut feeling is the same as reality. This intuition, instinct, prescience, whatever it is, proves to be prophetic so often its uncanny. While the young broker should have a working knowledge of how scientific methods are applied to the investment process, he should maintain a balance with the "art" of investing.

FWIW # 80 .... Cycles

Everything in the universe operates in cycles. While he is still in training, the young broker should begin studying stock market cycles. History does repeat itself in investing as in anything where human behavior is a factor. A word of caution is in order here. Cycles are not precise.

Just because a certain cycle is identified as being a nine year cycle does not mean it always recurs exactly every nine years. It does mean that, based on a number of recurrances, the average length of the cycle in question has been determined to be about nine years, give or take a few months.

Whenever a broker looks at an investment's potential he should study its price history over the long term. In this manner, he can discover what cycles have been identified. By studying these cyclical patterns in relation to the profitability of the corporation, the broker can begin to understand the inner rhythm of the investment.

Cycles hold one of the keys to successful investing.

MY WAY

FWIW # 81 .... **Hurdles**

To accumulate real wealth, an investor must overcome two major hurdles, inflation and taxation. Inflation is the same kind of obstacle as taxation, only more insidious because it affects before and after tax dollars. It is important for the broker to minimize his client's taxes while maintaining his flexibility so that inflation does not negate his gains.

One important strategy at the broker's disposal is to structure major investments according to the tax status of the investor and his family members. For example, he can put investments with tax free income in the name of the investor in a high tax bracket while putting investments with taxable income in the names of the investor's children or in his IRA account.

Whenever a young broker works with a client, he should always measure the potential return

MY WAY

from each investment being considered against the two hurdles of taxation and inflation.

FWIW # 82 ....Different Perspective

Try to imagine the following phone call:

Real Estate Broker: "Mr. (*Name*), This is Ricky Real with Land Realty. There is a great piece of real estate on 10th Street which is just right for you. It could double in price and you should buy it before it does."

Real Estate Client: "Sounds fine to me. Go ahead and get it. I'll send a check."

Or this one:

Real Estate Client: "Ricky, this is Mr. (*Name*), I have just learned that interest rates have risen and should rise some more. Please sell my land on 10th Street at whatever price you can get."

Or this one:

Real Estate Client: "Ricky, this is Mr. (*Name*). What is the price of my land on 10th Street this week and what was it last week?"

Of course, none of these conversations is likely to happen since the mindset of an investor dealing in real estate is different from that of an investor dealing in securities. A typical investor would not dream of buying a piece of real estate without looking it over carefully, and in some cases, having an outside, independent appraisal made. Yet the same investor will purchase common stocks or debentures on a whim or with only a cursory review of their "vital" statistics. Very rarely will he put the same effort into reviewing a security that he puts into inspecting real estate.

Only rarely does an investor pay 100% of the purchase price of a piece of real estate. As a rule of fact, he attempts to leverage his purchase as much as possible, even to the point of having negative cash flow. Yet the same investor probably does not make it a practice to buy securities with leverage, nor would he be willing to support a negative cash flow from his stock purchases.

When interest rates rise, all investments become less liquid and temporarily decline in value, if for no other reason than a higher expectation of discounted cash flow. The real estate investor does not worry about liquidating his investment as interest rates go up and the value of real estate declines. Yet, he thinks nothing of liquidating his stock or bond portfolio and congratulates himself for being so smart.

The real estate investor never really knows exactly what his investment is worth. All he really knows is what he paid for it. Because he does not see his property fluctuating in value from day to day, he is not subject to fits of anxiety over it. But the same investor calls his broker daily or weekly agonizing over every price change that has occurred and demanding to know the cause for it. He is concerned if a financially sound business enterprise goes bankrupt due to a weak economy, but gives no thought to the fact that the same

MY WAY

147

MY WAY

economic factors also cause the price of real estate to decline.

The point of these comparisons is that investors have differing perspectives on investments in real estate and securities. Real estate investors accept illiquidity and invest for the long term. It is not unusual for an investor to hold a piece of real e-state for five or ten years, dutifully·shelling out money for interest, taxes, maintenance, and insurance. As a matter of fact, a quick sale could result in adverse tax consequences. But the same investor, even though he has no tax implications other than long term capital gains, begins to think about liquidating his securities almost from the time he buys them simply because there is always a market for them and because he can sell them by making just one phone call.

If investors would only invest in the stock market with the same attitudes they have when investing in real estate, they would achieve equally good results. The broker has a responsibility to assist his clients in understanding the principles of successful investing. If the broker guides his client and helps him set parameters for investing, the client will have more assets to place under the broker's control.

By letting the liquidity, portability, and low cost of the securities markets work for his client, the broker can achieve the highest possible risk/ reward ratio.

FWIW # 83 ....Market Guarantee

The only prediction about the stock market that can be made with any degree of certainty is that it will always fluctuate. For the investor seeking long term capital gains, this fluctuation is actually the strength of the market. A young broker who understands this realizes that declining days in the market do not mean that the end of the world is at hand. He realizes that the only significance of another "down day" in the market is that the market is closer to "bottoming out" than it was the day before.

MY WAY

FWIW # 84 .... Too High/Too Low

According to the old cliche, an investor should buy low and sell high. The problem is in knowing what is high and what is low. The answer depends upon the individual.

The price of an investment is too low when the investor cannot sleep at night or function properly during the day because he is worrying that the price will rise before he purchases it.

The price of an investment is too high when the investor cannot sleep at night or function properly in the daytime because he is worrying that the price will decline before he takes his profit.

FWIW # 85 .... Top Priority

What is the absolute top criterion for choosing an investment to meet the objective of capital gains?

Price movement. As a broker reviews an investment he should make sure it will give the investor the possibility of significant capital gains. There are two ways to assess this critical factor.

When reviewing mature companies with cyclical earnings, the broker should review the

MY WAY

annual highs and lows for the past ten years to see how the price of the stock has reacted to various stages in the economic cycle. If the average annual high is only 20% above the average annual low, the broker must determine if any factor could cause this year to be different.

When reviewing companies with growing earnings, the broker must determine the market's perception of the earnings growth, and whether the rate of that growth will allow the price/earnings ratio to remain the same or expand.

Price movement is critical. The young broker must not overlook it when selecting investments.

FWIW # 86 .... Relatively Speaking

From the start, the young broker must understand that investment decisions cannot be made in a vacuum. When evaluating one investment, he must look at its strength and weaknesses in comparison to all available investments. The starting point for this comparison is the "risk free" rate of return. The classic example of the "risk free" investment is the 90 day U. S. Treasury Bill. The term "risk free" is used not only because a permanent loss of capital is not possible but also because changes in interest rates cannot cause a significant temporary loss of capital and/or liquidity.

From the riskless end of the investment spectrum, every other investment carries increasingly higher indicated rates of return, as well as increasingly higher degrees of risk. One of the broker's functions is to help the client identify his investment objectives and *risk taking* desires for the

MY WAY

funds in question. All investors have different monies for which they have varying risk acceptance levels. Once the risk quotient is identified, the broker can then present investments which fall within the acceptable level and meet his client's income and capital gains objectives.

The young broker will see the importance of understanding the relative value of investments when one security offers a potential return out of proportion to the apparent risk being accepted. Since the market place is fairly efficient, that is to say, quickly assigns value to all available information, unless he looks at all investments relatively, the young broker cannot fully understand the risks he is taking. For this reason, the broker should sit down once a month and list the investments offered by his firm on a legal pad divided into four columns. The investment name goes in the first column. The definite yield in the form of interest or dividends goes in the second column. The expected yield to be received through capital gains belongs in the third column. The potential risks of the investments belongs in the fourth column. The fourth column is bound to be highly subjective. The broker should be both conservative and consistant in his evaluations. There are three risk categories, credit risk, inflation risk, and illiquidity. While the first two risk categories are objective and can be applied to all investments for all investors, the last must be individually tailored to each investor.

The young broker must realize it is difficult for him to maintain a proper perspective on value since he must focus on one investment or one investor at a time. Unless he takes a portfolio management viewpoint, he will have difficulty adhering to the relative value concept.

MY WAY

FWIW # 87 .... Bad Marriages

There was a time when investment decisions, like marriage decisions, were made only once. A stock was purchased and kept forever because it generally went up year after year. Then came 1929 and 1968. Since 1968, stocks have had periods of profits and losses. The young broker should remember that *every investment* has a *buy price* and a *sell price*. In particular, the broker should avoid getting carried away emotionally to the point he "marries" a stock and cannot be objective in his viewpoint. Sometime in the future one-decision investing may again be possible. Even in that environment however, some investments will warrant selling because of speculative excesses.

Once a recommendation has reached the level of profit and loss predetermined by the broker at the time of purchase, the broker should begin to review the investment *relative* to other alternatives. There may also come a time when the price is too high, (FWIW # 84). If the broker's presentation was professional, his client will see the merit of selling to purchase another investment with greater relative value.

Client complaints about brokers' failures to tell them when to sell investments are second only to client complaints about losses. Having to watch a correct decision to buy turn into a bad investment because of a bad decision to sell gets very tiresome for both brokers and clients.

FWIW # 88 .... Patience

Because he is driven to earn commissions and

because the securities industry is a constantly changing environment, the hardest discipline for the young broker to learn is the patience to allow his recommendations to his clients to develop. Patience is more than the ability to wait until settlement date or until long-term capital gains are achieved. Patience is the ability to hold an investment through an entire economic cycle or the long-term recovery of a corporation. Patience is the *only* characteristic common to all successful investors.

How does the young broker reconcile the need to be patient with the need to make commission - generating transactions? Simply by recognizing the need to constantly and aggressively prospect not only for new clients but also for new money from existing clients.

FWIW # 89 .. The Obvious and the Exception

The successful investor looks beyond the obvious to find the obscure asset, fault, or trend which does not become apparent to others until a later time and a higher price. The only way for the young broker to make these discoveries is to ask "WHY?" and "WHAT IF?" when reviewing information about an investment. By examining various hypothetical scenarios, the young broker will begin to develop the perspective necessary for him to make intelligent investment decisions.

Another aspect of market insight is awareness of deviations from the norm. This awareness is essential for recognizing trends early. A course of events that does not proceed according to the laws of cause and effect should signal the broker that something is in the wind. A quarterly report

MY WAY

MY WAY

reflecting a sharp drop in earnings or a report of a quarterly loss without any correspsonding reaction in the price of the stock is abnormal. A world event that should cause the price of gold to rise but which has exactly the opposite effect also warrants closer investigation.

When a young broker is looking for fresh ideas in a difficult market, he should look at the new high list on days of large declines in the market.

By the same token, the new low list in a sharply rising market indicates likely candidates for put buying.

An awareness of events that are anything out of the ordinary and an ability to penetrate the obvious are traits which will enable the young broker to increase his chances for success.

FWIW # 90 ....Don't Play God

The young broker has a tendency to want to protect investors from making mistakes in buying securities. According to the young broker, a mistake is any opinion that differs from what he has learned to date or any investment decision that fails to fall in line with his firm's current recommendations. Every day a young broker will talk an investor out of doing what he really wanted to do and into another investment. When the young broker plays God like this, his chances of winning the client's confidence is poor. If the investment the client wanted to buy goes up more than the one the broker sold him, the client is unhappy. If the investment the client purchased goes down, he is unhappy. The only chance the broker has for the client to be happy is for the broker's recommendation to go up in value more than the client's original idea. One chance in three are not good odds. Playing God is a no win situation for a broker.

When a client contacts a broker and wants to buy a security which the broker thinks is inappropriate, it is incumbent upon the broker to explain the risks fully to the client. After assuring himself the client is fully aware of the risks he is taking, the broker must make a decision. If the investment is clearly unsuitable for the client the broker must decline to handle the transaction. Brokers who transact clearly unsuitable, unsolicited purchases are just as liable under Rule 405, Know Your Client Rule, as they are for solicited trades. If the client understands the risk and can afford to take the risk, the broker should allow him to go ahead with it.

FWIW # 91 .... Self-Styled Analyst

There is a kind of broker who tries to personally conduct in-depth research on every company he comes across before selling the security to his clients. This self-styled analyst does not realize the harm he is doing to his career. If he were really honest with himself, the self-styled analyst would realize his obsession with researching his own information has its roots in insecurity and fear of rejection. By "researching" before presenting to clients, the broker can keep busy "legitimately" without being productive.

The self-styled analyst assumes the role of unofficial critic of his firm's investment offerings. He takes it upon himself to uncover all of the negative aspects of the investment and then refuses to present the investment to his clients.

MY WAY

MY WAY

While he thinks he is saving his client from making a bad financial mistake, he is really doing his client a disservice, and destroying his own career.

Being a self-styled analyst is another way of playing God. No human being can do it successfully for long.

FWIW # 92.................................. Mindless Fool

Just as the self-styled analyst represents one extreme, the mindless fool represents the other. He has no critical faculties and no opinions of his own, and he is only too happy to have others do all of his thinking for him. The mindless fool shovels out any and all investments offered by his firm. Such a broker usually has a short career. Since he always relies on others to tell him what and when to buy, he never knows what or when to sell. Inevitably, his clients are left holding his recommendations when they go bad.

The broker's basic function is to bring together a client and his investment objective with the investment which *best* meets that objective (and which may or may not be whatever his firm is currently promoting). The broker must therefore know not only his clients, but also the features and benefits of the investments available to them.

FWIW # 93 .... Buy the Whole Company

Anyone who overheard a conversation between the typical young broker and his client would probably think that they were playing a new board game or acting out a parody for a TV comedy show. They talk about technical patterns and analysis, about takeovers, rumors, and inside tips from you-know-who. They discuss support and resistance levels as if they were tangible, concrete entities instead of theoretical constructs. The only topic missing from the discussion is an evaluation of what the company is worth. If the investor is going to pay for the earnings, cash flow, and assets of any viable concern, he should know more about what he's buying than the price and movement charts alone can tell him. He would not agree to purchase the local drugstore, hardware store, or corner grocery store without so much as a glance at its balance sheets. Why, then, would he be willing to buy shares of stock in a company without knowing anything about its assets and liabilities?

"Looking to buy the whole company" simply means that a businessman's perspective is brought to bear on investment decisions. The young broker who raises the question of total value will not only help his client to make better investment decisions, but will also upgrade his professional image in the eyes of his client.

FWIW # 94 .... Tax Knowledge

The young stockbroker is forbidden to give tax advice to his clients. However, the professional broker must know every aspect of the tax laws. This point cannot be over stressed. Investments such as tax shelters, original issue bonds, nine month options, and common stocks have special treatment under tax laws. Depending on the client's tax situation, any investment can change from an asset to a liability.

MY WAY

A thorough knowledge of taxes takes a great deal of time. Educational study should come after normal business hours. This commitment of time he spends will be rewarded by the young broker's client's increased perception of his professionalism. The broker should refer the prospect/client to his tax attorney or CPA with specific questions. If the broker is confident of his facts, he can address the issue with his client in this manner.

"Mr. (*Name*), while I am not a CPA or tax attorney and I do not profess to give tax advice, it would be to your benefit to discuss with your tax advisor the fact that under certain circumstances an operating corporation can accumulate up to $250,000 worth of another domestic corporation's stock and receive a dividend payment from those stocks 85% tax free. If you like, the three of us could have a conference call and go over the investment tax ramifications strategy you and I have discussed."

Approaching the client in such a manner enables the broker to steer toward the right investment decision based on tax considerations. Unless he has extensive knowledge of the tax code, a young broker does not know how to focus on the tax benefits of the investment. The young broker should be careful not to make the tax advisor to look less than professional for not having advised the client on the subject before. By handling himself properly, the young broker may impress the tax advisor and develop an influential source of referrals.

FWIW # 95 ...... Factors in Decision Making

Every research report is a mixture of fact and

opinion. A young broker can learn a great deal about investment markets by studying research reports and seeing how various analysts interpret facts. For each stock he follows, the young broker should keep a log of features and how each influences a particular stock, industry, or the overall market. Since there are innumerable factors which can effect the overall market or, for that matter, an individual stock, it may take years to fit some of the pieces together. What the young broker must keep in mind is that he does not need to have every single piece of the puzzle in order to get a clear picture. Because the young broker plans to make the brokerage business his life's work, it behooves him to learn as much as possible about how to keep and make money.

MY WAY

FWIW # 96 .... Serious Money

Serious money is defined as that money which an investor has committed to the investment markets for the long term. The investor is willing to reinvest all income and profits to accelerate the growth of his capital. He does not withdraw serious money to buy a new car, to take a trip to Europe, or even to put a child through college. Serious money is money which has the sole objective of making more money through capital gains and reinvestment of income.

Ideally, a young broker's main objective will be to open accounts funded by serious money. Of course, as he prospects he will open any and all accounts possible. As his business progresses, however, the young broker should train his sales assistant to handle those accounts which do not represent serious money.

MY WAY

Finally, the young broker should be willing to handle an account of any size as long as it represents serious money. He should ask for a certain minimum amount, for example $25,000 equity in a margin account, but be willing to search out the amount of serious money the prospect has and accept at least that amount. If the broker is professional in his investment knowledge and if the broker concentrates on serious money, this pool of serious money will grow and so will the broker's production and income.

FWIW # 97 .... Managing Money

The typical young broker thinks that proper investment management techniques can be applied to only large portfolios. Nothing could be further from the truth. When a broker has "serious money" to invest he should use a money management concept even if the amount is small. If the investment philosophy calls for utilizing ten investment units, the fund should be spread over those ten units whether the total is $5,000, $50,000, or $500,000. Obviously, the larger units can utilize listed options where the smaller units cannot. This, however, is the only difference.

Within the confines of investment units, a suggested equity portfolio can be diversified with 70% of its assets in big capitalization stocks carrying listed options, 20% in smaller growth stocks, and 10% in truly high risk "special" situations.

The logic behind this distribution of assets into equity groups is simple. First, the preservation of capital is a prerequisite to the accumulation of wealth. By investing 70% of equity money in big capitalization stocks carrying listed options, an investor should be able to ride out market swings while generating a 10% cash return annually through dividends and option premiums. At the same time, good timing should add a small amount of capital gains on a regular basis.

By investing 20% of his capital in small growth-oriented companies, the investor should be able to keep significant returns on the total portfolio. His winners in this category should return 300% or more in the long run. The return depends heavily upon the investor's willingness to cut his losses short.

Every young broker and investor dreams of finding the cheap stock which rises to a high price, giving returns of ten to one or more. The average investor tends to allocate too much of his money to such situations, not realizing he is putting himself in danger. By risking the majority of his capital, he stands to lose everything. Because the potential returns are so enormous, an investor can achieve significant results without risking more than 10% of his total capital on highly speculative investments. By utilizing the tax deduction for capital losses to offset gains elsewhere, the young broker and his client should be able to make steady progress toward their goal of increasing the "serious money" in the client's account.

Stock picking is standing in one place and being lucky enough for it to be the right place. Managing money is using the dynamics of the economy, the market place, and individual stocks to preserve and increase a client's capital base.

FWIW # 98 .... In-House Research

When it comes to taking abuse from the bro-

MY WAY

MY WAY

kers, the firm's Research Department is second only to the Operations Department. When questioned about why, the broker cites frustration with analysts' seemingly senseless opinions and changes of opinions, both of which are usually wrong. The cause of this frustration lies more in the broker's ignorance of investment principles and stock selection than the analyst's advice. Naturally, if the broker relies upon the analyst to recommend purchasing a security then he also relies on the analyst to give him a sell signal. Analysts almost never do that. Disappointments arise as the broker watches profits dwindle and the analyst writes longer and longer reports on why the security should be going up and not down. One of the cardinal rules on proper use of a firm's Research Department is to sell stock holdings when the analyst issues frequent and defensive reports on the company. A good recommendation does not need to be constantly defended.

A Research Department, properly utilized, can become a major asset for the broker. He must, however, realize that the analyst is human and fallible, and that his information consists of opinions which may be wrong. It is up to the broker to evaluate each analyst individually and to determine if there is any consistency to his performance.

The broker wants the analyst to be a confirming factor within his core group of stocks, (FWIW # 101). The analyst should be a check on the validity of the broker's reasons for positioning the stock. If there are differences of opinion, the broker can zero in on these differences and make judgements as to who is correct on each point. For other securities in which the broker or his client has an interest, the broker acts as inquisitor and reviews the logic of the analysts' facts and opinions. One of the best tools a broker has at his disposal is an alphabetized, flat, letter-size file folder. This folder has a backbone that expands like an accordian, usually with 21 sections marked A-Z. As he receives research reports, the broker files them under the appropriate letter. If a prospect/client makes an inquiry, the broker has only to open his file to the appropriate place to see if his Research Department has published any information on the subject. In this time of electronic communication, the broker may have to assign his sales assistant the permanent assignment of making copies of these reports each day. While one of the benefits of the research file is that it enables the broker to answer inquiries about securities quickly and knowledgeably, its real value comes after a year or two when it enables the broker to track an analyst's reports against a security's price action. Only then can the broker make a fair assessment of the analyst and, more importantly, decide how to utilize his reports.

An analyst who is consistently wrong is just as valuable as one who is consistently right. The erratic analyst is the difficult one to deal with. By comparing reports written over a period of time, the broker will begin to pick up the subtle changes in wording which generally mean the analyst is beginning to have doubts about a position he has taken.

Technical analysis is different from fundamental analysis. The broker must realize that technical analysis is an art. Just as a world class skeet shooter occasionally misses, a technical analyst will occasionally misinterpret the chart

163

MY WAY

patterns. There will be times when the analyst is very good at calling market conditions and short term stock price movements, and times when the same analyst cannot function profitably at all. For this reason, the broker should have two or three sources of technical advice. Naturally, he should develop a certain level of skill himself so he can make his own calls when the analysts disagree. The broker should keep this axiom in mind:

"The longer a technician has been right, the closer he is to being wrong. The same goes for being wrong." Technical analysis is a self-fulfilling prophesy at best and sheer guess work at worst.

In summary, a broker should look upon his firm's Research Department as a tool and not a source. Having access to in-house research does not eliminate the need for the broker to use his own common sense in selecting investments, or in investing, but it can help to reduce his potential mistakes to the lowest possible number.

FWIW # 99 .... No Research Department

Some brokerage firms have no Research Department, good or bad. To generate good investment ideas, the young broker at such a firm must "hire" his own research analysts. While his first thought may be to subscribe to market letters, it is not recommended. The subscriber to a market letter generally gets many opinions and very few facts. Instead, the young broker's first step should be to buy some good books on technical analysis and subscribe to a chart service. It is important for the broker to keep notes on how he interprets the charts and compare his notes with how stock price movement unfolds. Only in this fashion can he learn from his bad calls and improve his ability to "read" charts as time goes on.

Most mutual fund organizations have access to diverse sources of research. The broker can take advantage of the situation. First, by determining what mutual funds have roughly the same investment philosophy he does, and then by studying their holdings in a current prospectus. While this method of identifying opportunities may not seem timely, most good investments take years to work out. In addition, the broker can make purchases on pull backs.

Some, but not all, investment magazines offer good investment ideas. The young broker should take care to avoid "fad" stocks, which are overpriced due to the unusual amount of publicity they receive.

A simple method of searching out stock ideas is to review the market pages in the morning paper. Which stocks are making new lows? Which are making new highs? Which stocks indicate wide trading patterns? Which stocks pay high dividends? The broker should select names and send for free annual reports so he may pursue his investigations.

A broker who is aware of what is going on around him should never be at a loss for investment ideas. No matter what the idea may be, the very least he can do is to go to the library and study subscription reports the library receives. A Research Department is not necessary for the broker who is constantly thinking about his business as he goes about his daily activities.

MY WAY

MY WAY

FWIW # 100 ..... Reading a Research Report

No matter where the young broker gets his research material, he must learn to read it properly. Each research report should contain three key elements: (1) facts, (2) reasoning, and (3) opinions or conclusions. The young broker's first step should be to extract all factual information and list it, point by point, on a piece of paper. He can now translate each positive feature into a benefit for the prospect/client, and, at the same time, develop responses to objections elicited by negative facts or features. The listing of the negative facts enables the broker to assess just how much fundamental risk is involved with the purchase of the particular security.

Since everyone does not look at a company the same way, the broker, by reading research reports on the same company by different analysts, will be able to assemble facts like pieces of a jigsaw puzzle. The information he gathers over a period of time from several sources will be greater than that from any single source, and, should therefore, make for a clearer picture than would otherwise be available to him.

The broker will find it easier to assess the validity of an analyst's conclusions if he first studies the kind of reasoning the analyst used to interpret the data. In time, he will come to notice whenever an analyst has forced the facts to fit his opinion rather than the other way around. This kind of knowledge will help the broker avoid some investment mistakes, and, therefore, assist in building his confidence as his career progresses.

By the time the broker has enumerated the facts and identified the logic used by the ananlyst in reaching his conclusions, he should be able to form his own opinion. If it is the same as the analyst's opinion, that is great. If it isn't, the broker should ignore the analyst's opinion since the analyst has nothing to lose in any impending transaction. The broker, on the other hand, has worked hard prospecting to get the client and has his reputation as an investment professional at stake. He must live with the consequences of the trade, good or bad, and he knows it. If he is doing his homework and progressing in all aspects of his profession, his own "intuition" will steer him right most of the time.

MY WAY

FWIW # 101 .... **Merchandising**

It is the exceptional young broker who looks at himself as an entrepreneur. The broker who sees himself as a retailer or merchandiser is even more of a rarity. Yet, aren't his clients members of the investing public? The retail broker does attempt to satisfy the needs and wants of the investing public. Therefore, he is a retailer. It follows that since his clientele is diverse, a broker should have knowledge of each investment category offered by his firm. This is true even for a broker who specializes in one investment area.

So that he can have easy access to his information when assisting a client, the young broker should establish file folders in his desk for each investment category. For example, he may want to make folders for insurance, real estate, precious metals, venture capital, oil and gas, and collateral-backed obligations. The categories can be as broad or as detailed as the broker desires.

The young broker should accumulate the latest information on each offering within the appro-

MY WAY

priate folder so that he is always ready to assist a prospect/client who has an inquiry. The broker should take each folder home occasionally to study the contents and develop an approach to marketing that particular category of investment.

Another folder the young broker should have on his desk is one entitled "Fixed Income Opportunities." (See Sample) He should keep daily listings of bonds that he finds attractive at the time of issue in this folder. Under each heading the broker should list an issue taken from his firm's inventory sheet each day.

SAMPLE

DATE_____

FIXED INCOME OPPORTUNITIES

	Current Yield	YTM
U.S. TREASURY ISSUES:		
(1) 3 month bills:		
(2) 1 year note:		
(3) 5 year note:		
(4) 10 year bond:		
(5) 15 year bond:		
(6) 20 year bond:		
(7) 30 Year bond:		
(8) Zero CPN issue:		

	Current Yield	YTM
AAA ISSUES-TAXABLE:		
(1) 7 year maturity:		
(2) 15-20 year maturity:		
(3) Over 20 year maturity:		

	Current Yield	YTM	MY WAY
AAA ISSUES-NONTAXABLE:			

AAA ISSUES-NONTAXABLE:

(1) 7 year maturity:
(2) 15-20 year maturity:
(3) Over 30 year maturity:

A RATED-TAXABLE:
(1) 7 year maturity:
(2) 15-20 year maturity:
(3) Over 20 year maturity:

A RATED-NONTAXABLE:
(1) 7 year maturity:
(2) 15-20 year maturity:
(3) Over 20 year maturity:

OTHER OPPORTUNITIES: _____
_____
_____
_____

This "Fixed Income Opportunities" folder should always be right where he needs it so that he can supply a client with a good investment without fumbling around or having to call the client back. An additional benefit is that the broker always knows the direction of the bond market and the shape of the yield curve. Eventually the listings come to serve as references showing past patterns of bond prices. The fixed income folder can become a powerful sales tool, because the broker can use it to show the client how prices have changed. Needless to say, completing the "Fixed Income Opportunities" listing takes more than a couple of minutes each day. Therefore, the broker

MY WAY

should perform this function before 9:30 a.m. and the earlier the better. As he goes through the bond offerings, the broker will begin to put clients' needs and wants together with available bonds and add to his daily list of scheduled calls.

The final merchandising category should be equities. Here again, the objective is for the broker to have a working knowledge of a select group of stocks which cover the entire macroeconomic spectrum. (See FWIW # 108) When a client requests a recommendation from a broker, the broker selects one of the "core" issues that he follows closely. This is not to say that if the client wants to purchase one stock, the broker will sell him another. (See FWIW # 90). Most of the time the client indicates to the broker a certain amount of money is available and requests a recommendation. As the broker's reputation grows, more and more of his clients will take this approach.

While the number of issues in a broker's "core" group of stocks can vary, the young broker should not attempt to follow more than twenty. As more of a young broker's prospects come from referrals and fewer from cold calls, he will have the time to increase the stocks in his "core" group. Naturally, the broker should get himself added to his core companies' financial mailing lists, and should keep research reports which deal with any of these stocks. He should position only three or four of these "core" stocks in his clients' accounts at any given time since they represent diverse cyclical industries.

Besides representing the twelve macroeconomic sectors of the economy, a young broker's "core" group of stocks should also be diversified into three categories: (1) big capitalization stocks, (2) small growth companies, and (3) special situations. He should apply the following guidelines in each category:

Big Capitalization Stocks: This category should definitely include each macroeconomic group and should constitute at least 70% of the "core" group. The emphasis should be on quality, name recognition, NYSE listing, and listed options. The high and low prices should exceed 50% annually.

Smaller Growth Stocks: These should be companies with revenues of $50,000,000 to $200,000,000 within growth industries. Here again, the emphasis should be on quality. Approximately 20% of the "core" group would fall within this category. Generally, these issues trade OTC or AMEX.

Special Situations: These issues should be dirt cheap because of a situation perceived to be negative. These are ultra high risk situations which should carry a minimum reward/risk ratio of five to one. Only 10% of the "core" group should fall into this classification.

Once the broker has selected his "core" group of stocks, he should not change any of the big capitalization issues or the small growth issues for several years. The "special situations" by their very nature will change constantly as the stocks either go bankrupt or work out to be profitable situations.

Having intelligently planned his coverage of the investment spectrum, the broker should be able to smoothly and intelligently present an investment opportunity to almost any prospect/client who has defined almost any investment objective. Even if the client prefers a situation other than the one offered by the broker, the broker's professional approach will instill confidence in the prospect/client.

MY WAY

MY WAY

FWIW # 102 .... Lo Price vs. Hi Price

Brokerage house studies indicate that many clients do not like a broker to recommend only low priced stocks. At the same time, if left to their own devices, an even larger number of clients would purchase nothing but low price stocks. There is no easy answer to the "problem" of human nature. The solution is for the broker to be flexible. Initially, however, the broker should recognize a new client's hesitancy to commit large sums of money to a new broker. Of course the broker has already asked the proper questions in order to establish the correct size investment unit. (See FWIW # 67). And naturally, he has selected a stock which will meet the client's investment objective. The broker's initial recommendation should start with a low price stock, the $15.00 to $20.00 range because in the client's mind it sets up an equation between an investment unit and a large number of shares. As the broker's recommendations develop profitably, the client will gradually become accustomed to owning more shares of higher priced stocks.

The broker should not buy stocks under $10.00 a share unless they belong in his small growth stock category or his special situation category. (See FWIW # 101). In other words, the stock will not stay in that price range for long.

FWIW # 103 .... The Devil in Us

No matter what their upbringing and no matter what they preach, all human beings have the desire to gamble or speculate for the fast buck or get rich quick scheme. A professional broker

172

will recognize this fact and be prepared to deal with it in order to keep a client.

There are two golden rules to speculating. First, the payoff must be well worth the risk. If the risk is 100%, the potential reward should be at least 500%. Second, a speculator cannot play the game unless he has the price of admission, i.e., money. It makes no sense for anyone to risk all or a large part of his capital on one speculative venture. If the reward/risk relationship is at least 500%, a small amount of money can bring a handsome return. Since speculations are long shots, and since long shots are seldom successful, or they would not be classified as such, the speculator must be willing to accept a series of small losses. By risking only a small amount on any given trade, the speculator can stay around for the potential payoff.

In summary, the young broker must realize that everyone likes to speculate sometimes, and he needs to know how to guide his clients through the process of speculating intelligently.

FWIW # 104 ...Trading - The Good and Bad

While an active stock and option trader is every young broker's dream, in reality, he soon becomes his nightmare. Successful short-term trading over a long period of time is very difficult for the Wall Street professional and nearly impossible for the retail client. A broker who builds his clientele with traders is building his career on a foundation of sand. It soon makes for sleepless nights. Either the trader starts to lose money, or, he becomes increasingly aware of the commissions generated by his transactions since they eat into his trading capital.

MY WAY

MY WAY

To maximize the benefits of having active traders during his career, the broker should recognize that the trader is not a permanent part of his business. When the account is opened, the broker should take a few minutes to establish clear lines of communication with the trader. His sales assistant should be party to this. Since traders who make their own decisions usually demand hefty discounts on commissions, the broker should establish in advance just how much time he will devote to the trader's account.

To handle these types of accounts in a professional manner, the broker must have a good knowledge of technical analysis and must give prompt and accurate executions. He should establish a rapport with either his wire operator or, if orders are entered by phone, with his firm's trading desk. If problems arise, the broker should monitor the situation carefully through his sales assistant. If for some reason there is not a quick resolution to the problem, the broker should enlist the aid of his operations manager or office manager.

The young broker should think of traders as the icing on a cake made up of good quality, long-term investors.

FWIW # 105 .... Buy Rumor/Sell News

A young broker must realize that the stock market is an anticipartory market. The stock market looks to the future and anticipates changes in economic and social events. As the event gets closer and attention is more sharply focused on it, market participants begin to adjust their investments to reflect their expectations of the outcome and its impact on the market. When the event finally takes place, only minor ripples go through the market. These ripples reflect positions taken by the public which *reacts* to the *actual* event taking place.Since the major market participants have already made their moves, the ripples never become big waves. Consequently, the reactive position of the public turns out to be a loss.

The exception to the normal anticipatory nature of the market comes when some totally unexpected, unpredicted, extraordinary event takes place. For example, if a world leader is assassinated and his replacement subscribes to a totally different economic philosophy. A surprise takeover announcement, or a large, unexpected quarterly loss can change the price of a stock just as suddenly. Such exceptions are just that: *exceptions* to a rule which states that traders should buy the rumor and sell the news.

FWIW # 106 .... Balanced Investing

In the traditional sense, investing encompasses cash, bonds, stocks, real estate, and gold. The percentage of each the young broker's client should own depends upon the client's personal circumstances and objectives. For clients who take a simplistic approach to investing, the total funds to be invested could be fairly evenly distributed, with 12.5% each in cash and gold and 25% each in bonds, stocks and real estate. As the relative value of each group changes, the overvalued group can be reduced to its starting level, and the proceeds from liquidation can be invested in the undervalued asset group.

This process is called formula or balanced

MY WAY

investing. Given the assumption that each investment will eventually come into fashion, the discipline of selling overvalued assets makes sense. Problems arise when an investment category does not come into vogue or the overvalued asset group continues to go up.

FWIW # 107 .... Being a Contrarian

Ever since Bernard Baruch sat on a park bench and explained his investment philosophy by saying he bought his straw hats in the winter, most investors have paid lip service to the notion of being a contrarian. It is not normal human behavior to go against the crowd so investors tend to rationalize and to make up their own "revised" definitions of what constitutes contrary investing. When traders eagerly await the publication of a contrary opinion index, has the contrary opinion not become the popular opinion?

Being a contrarian does not mean an investor merely buys whatever is down in price. Being a contrarian means searching through seriously endangered investments, such as companies in or near bankruptcy, to find those who have the management, franchise, or assets which may keep them from going under and pull them through their difficulties - perhaps. Being a contrarian means sticking to an investment position when everyone else is convinced that one financial path is wrong and that the correct path is clearly marked.

Opportunities for being a contrarian do not arise every day. Usually there are only a few special situations which become available each year. This is good since it enables the broker to build a large position in the stocks of his choice.

Finally, the true test of whether a security qualifies as a contrary opinion stock is to ask other brokers and clients what they think of it. If their reply is, "Are you crazy? There is no way that dog will ever come back," it passes.

MY WAY

FWIW # 108 .... Macroeconomic Groups

As mentioned in FWIW # 101, for a broker to be able to offer an equity investment which has merit to his clients at any time and in any economic environment, he needs to have a core group of stocks representing the whole economy. In investing, it is generally accepted that the economy can be separated into macroeconomic groups. One such grouping breakdown is as follows:

(1) Basic Industries
(2) Technology
(3) Capital Investment
(4) Multi-Industry
(5) Consumer Growth
(6) Consumer Cyclicals
(7) Defensive Consumer
(8) Interest Cyclicals
(9) Oil & Gas
(10) Banking Services
(11) Transportation
(12) Utilities

As can be seen, the "macro" aspect of each sector is huge. Within each sector are tens of industries and hundreds of stocks. The young broker quickly realizes that if he is going to develop substantial knowledge on a few issues, he has some tough decisions to make. This de-

MY WAY

cision making process is in itself a discipline since each decision is one of relative value.

Even though a young broker is inclined to prefer one sector to another, there are two strong reasons for including representatives from all twelve in his core group. First, due to the cyclical nature of the economy, one sector may be up while another is down and the rest are moving from one extreme to another. If his core stocks are spread among all twelve sectors, the young broker always has an opportunity to recommend a good value to his prospect/client, no matter what the state of the economy. Second, investors have their own pet theories about buying stocks. With a group of stocks from every sector of the economy, the young broker can always give the prospect/client what he wants.

FWIW # 109 ... Retirement Account Investing

Retirement accounts are the young broker's future. It is important for the young broker to realize there is a difference between successful investment management for retirement accounts and taxable accounts management. To go back to basics, there are two hurdles to overcome in successful investing, (1) taxation, and (2) inflation. With a tax-deferred retirement account, an investor has eliminated one of the two roadblocks to accumulating wealth. The only hurdle left is inflation.

Taking another perspective, there are only two methods to have capital generate more capital: (1) through income in the form of dividends, interest, or rents, and (2) through capital gains. In a taxable situation, dividends and other income

MY WAY

items are penalized through a higher tax rate. In addition, capital gains must be taken after a specified period of time in order to obtain favorable tax treatment. Consequently, a great many decisions concerning investments are made for reasons other than because they make good investment sense. In a retirement account, all of these hinderances to making money are eliminated. That is what makes these accounts so important to young brokers and their prospects/clients. Pure investment decisions can be made in the retirement account.

The fact that the tax aspects of investment management in a retirement account have been eliminated also reduces the impact of inflation. The young broker must examine the long term rate of inflation in order to understand why this is so. While inflation can run into double digits in the short-term, the long-term rate is substantially less than 10%. Since no tax is paid on income produced in a retirement account, the investments can be managed to set up a significant cash flow each year. This cash flow should assist the account to outstrip inflation in the long-term while capital gains and compounding of cash flow should add to the real wealth of the account.

The structured cash flow from dividends and interest provides an additional advantage. As time goes on and the value of the account increases, the size of this cash flow also increases significantly. As the economy goes through many cycles, interest rates and inflation rise and fall. When interest rates are rising, fixed income investments, and, at times, equity investments fall in value. The significant cash flow from investments, can be employed to make investments at these lower prices thus eliminating the necessity

MY WAY

of waiting for future contributions. Another advantage lies in the retirement account's ability to use its cash flow for unexpected withdrawals thus avoiding the untimely liquidation of assets.

For the broker to structure the investments in a retirement account, he must have comprehensive knowledge of the actual plan and data on the participants. The first thing the broker must consider is the nature of the plan. Is the plan a defined benefit or defined contribution plan? With a defined benefit plan, there is a certain amount of liability on the part of the corporation to make sure sufficient funds will be available to provide the stated benefits upon the participant's retirement. Consequently, these plans lean toward insurance and other fixed income investments with stated maturity values. A defined contribution plan is designed to provide each participant with a pool of money upon retirement. This pool of money is then reinvested to generate retirement income. In either case, there is significant fiduciary responsibility imposed on all trustees, administrators, and investment managers to invest the money prudently.

The second factor the broker must consider is the ages of the major participants. Retirement of a major participant,or for that matter, of all of the major participants, occurs on a predetermined date. The plan should have ample funds available at that time so that forced liquidation of assets is unnecessary.

The third factor the broker must consider is the attitude of the trustees. Ideally, the trustees allow a broad spectrum of investments based upon proper investment management principles. Regretably, that is not always the case. When the trustees want to interfere and set investment parameters, the young broker had better remember that it's their money and they have a right to set those parameters. If the young broker believes the plan should follow a certain investment strategy, he should make his recommendation in writing to the trustees. If the young broker's recommendations prove to be sound ones, the trustees should eventually gain confidence in him.

The starting point for the allocation of assets between fixed income and equities is, of course, 50%-50%. Adjustments must be made for the economic outlook and a whole host of other factors in addition to those already discussed. (Since the structure of a fixed income portfolio is the same for all investors, FWIW # 112 will cover the construction of a fixed income portfolio.)

Cash flow is important in a retirement account, even in the equity portion. For this reason, a self-imposed cash flow discipline is recommended. This discipline should be one-half the 90 day T-Bill rate. This does not mean that every stock purchased must yield exactly this amount, but it does mean that if the broker wants to place an investment unit in a stock with a lower yield, he must place another investment unit in a stock with a correspondingly higher yield to compensate. This self-imposed discipline of keeping yields equal to half of the 90 day T-Bill rate keeps the broker from making a lot of mistakes when the euphoria of a Bull Market has everyone believing the market will keep going up indefinitely. Not only is it a good investment strategy, but the discipline is also a strong selling point that most trustees will respond to favorably because it makes good sense to them.

FWIW # 97, Managing Money, outlines the approach which should be taken in equity man-

MY WAY

181

MY WAY

agement. In cases where the client desires to participate in the area of real estate,the young broker can use either common stocks of real estate companies or real estate limited partnerships. The choice really depends upon the amount of liquidity desired. Common stocks of real estate companies offer a degree of liquidity not found in limited partnerships.

With so many professionals going after the same dollars, it is not easy for a broker to compete for retirement accounts. It is recommended the broker use the cold calling process already outlined, (FWIW # 69), to ask for an appointment. The young broker's initial appointment should have a double objective: (1) get to see plan assets and information, and (2) get to make a formal presentation to the decision maker. The young broker could make his request in this manner:

"Mr. (*Name*), your business is _____ and mine is investments. Obviously you are a professional in your field and would want a professional to manage the valuable assets you are investing for your future. To enable you to have an indepth review of your present investment strategy, I am requesting the opportunity to make a formal presentation to you and whatever group you choose. This presentation takes less than one hour and carries with it a significant benefit to you, *no matter what decision you make afterward*. That benefit is that you will leave the meeting with a much clearer understanding of how a retirement account should be managed so that assets are protected and significant returns are possible. When could we go through this educational process?"

While the young broker is making the appointment for the formal presentation, it's a simple

182

matter to request a list of current assets for the purpose of developing the presentation. Once he has that, he has accomplished his dual objectives of the initial meeting. If the young broker prepares properly, makes his presentation in a professional manner, and is both patient and persistant, he will eventually obtain the account.

MY WAY

FWIW # 110 . . . . Margin

One of the most misunderstood and misused tools in the brokerage business is the margin account. While it is acceptable to use leverage, (borrowed money), for buying anything from automobiles to boats to businesses to residences, the memories and the stories of the Crash of '29 still prejudice equity investors against using leverage to buy securities. More often than not, those who do use margin use it incorrectly and end up with their equity wiped out or severely impaired. This does nothing to improve an already bad reputation. The broker who takes the time to understand the mechanics of margin and its proper role in investment strategy will be able to assist his clients in increasing their net worth even as he increases his commissions.

Any discussion of margin must begin with the tax structure and the individual investor. As of this writing, a certain portion of investment interest expense may be deducted from ordinary income. For the investor in the 50% tax bracket who can deduct the full amount from his income, this means that the *actual* rate of interest is only *half* of the quoted rate. If his selection of securities is a good one and he has long term capital gains, the investor ends up with a tax rate of only

MY WAY

20% (as opposed to the 50% he started out with). It is the difference in tax rates that makes margin accounts so attractive.

Before a full discussion of the benefits of using margin can take place, the dangers and pitfalls need to be understood. As of this writing, the loan value on marginable securities is 50%. An investor with $50,000 in cash can purchase $100,000 in stocks by borrowing $50,000. If he does this, the first problem a margin buyer can face is a decline in the price of his securities. When the equity in the account falls to 30% of the market value of the securities, the brokerage firm issues a margin call to restore the account to the required 50-50 balance. If the investor cannot put up the additional capital, securities will be sold to bring the account in balance.

The second problem a margin buyer can encounter is increasing interest rates. There are times when the interest rate will move so high that the total return on the client's investment is not sufficient to pay the interest charge on his loan. As rates go higher the interest charge erodes the equity. At the same time, the market value deteriorates because of higher interest rates. This slow wasting of assets eventually results in a margin call.

While the first two ways a margin investor can get in trouble are market-related, the third way has to do with poor judgement on the part of the investor and the broker. Typically, it begins with the deposit of stock or the purchase of investment grade securities. Once the securities are in the account, either the client or the broker decides to take advantage of "SMA" and make some "easy" money by purchasing some fast moving stock or option. The first few trades are invariably successful. The client thinks he has found the short cut to easy money and the broker thinks he is going to be a million dollar producer in no time. At that point, either the market cycle changes or the client's luck runs out. Whatever the reason, the stocks or options stop going up and the account becomes inflexible. If stocks were used to speculate, there is the slim consolation of holding them for years in the hope that they will recover. The most serious damage to the account occurs when the client has speculated on listed options. Neither the broker nor his client knows how quickly time can pass until he owns long option positions which have gone down or, worse, have declined in value because the underlying stock has not gone up. When options go against an investor, there is no tomorrow. Once options have expired, the money is gone forever.

The final danger of a margin account lies in a client's mistaken belief that he can utilize the "SMA" in the account for living expenses and let the rising value of his account overcome these withdrawals. Such a client ends up with memorable vacations, a nice boat or car, and nothing else.

The pitfalls of the margin account can be avoided if the broker and his client are sensible. The purpose of a margin account is two fold. First, keeping investments in a margin account reduces the need for maintaining substantial ready cash reserves. The margin account offers liquidity, so that cash reserves can be invested in one year CD's with higher yields than those offered by money market accounts. If an emergency or unexpected opportunity that's too good to pass up does arise, the "SMA" can be used until the CD matures.

MY WAY

MY WAY

The second purpose of a margin account is to enable the investor to purchase with borrowed funds investments which have the potential total returns of 40% to 50%. A good guideline is that the return on the investment should be at least three times the cost of the funds. When a client uses his equity to purchase securities, the broker should advise him to decide upon a stop-loss point in terms of the amount of equity to be risked. Once the client has determined the amount of equity he is willing to risk, this amount can be translated into a drop in the price of the stock.

Positions in a margin account should represent a highly diversified portfolio of stocks to reduce the potential for decline that exists in a heavily concentrated account often resulting in forced liquidations. While Reg. T of the Federal Reserve allows the purchase of two times the amount of marginable stock for each dollar of equity, the wise young broker starts off with a smaller debit balance. A prudent businessman does not utilize his entire line of credit.

Finally, dividends, interest, and any option premiums that are collected should be utilized to reduce the margin debit balance, and, therefore, reduce the interest expense.

While the young broker must learn the mechanics of the margin account in order to pass the broker registration exam, the typical young broker has no idea how to determine a margin account balance when he finishes with his training. This is unfortunate because the correct use of margin is one of the most important tools a successful broker has at his disposal. A young broker will find it is greatly to his benefit to get further instruction from his operations manager. The fact that the broker can get an updated margin balance from

the desk terminal does not diminish the importance of his knowing how to compute margin requirements manually. Sometimes the electron-
ically generated figures are wrong. If the client
uses those incorrect figures and suffers a loss
through market action before liquidation, it is the
client's loss and not the brokerage firm's. To be
professional the broker must be able to compute
margin requirements rapidly and accurately.

It is strongly recommended that every account
the young broker opens be a margin account. Just
because the use of borrowed funds is possible,
however, does not mean it is necessary or even
desirable. If the broker is prospecting for "guided accounts," (FWIW # 77), the brokerage accounts which have checks and debit cards would
be the natural accounts to open because they are
already margin accounts. For smaller accounts,
the young broker can incorporate the following
presentation into his account opening sequence:

"Mr. (*Name*), you have indicated a desire to
make your investments based upon sound investment management principles. In order to ensure
you the flexibility and liquidity necessary in case
of an emergency, the account you open will have
the capacity to become a margin account, if you
so decide."

It goes without saying that any account which
is opened with the intention of collecting option
premiums should be a margin account.

FWIW # 111 .. Fixed Income/Fixed Maturity

There use to be a clear distinction between
equities, which were considered speculative, and
fixed income/fixed maturity securities, common-

MY WAY

ly called bonds, which were considered safe within the credit risks of the issuing firms. When a client invested in equities, he joined a group in a speculative venture. When a client invested in bonds, he merely lent his money, usually as a secured creditor. Then along came the 1970's, rapid inflation, and floating interest rates. Bonds became as risky as equities. In some cases, it became apparent some equities appeared to be safer than bonds of good quality with long maturities and low coupon rates.

Until the day comes when interest rates will stabilize, (and that day *will* come), the young broker and his prospect/client need to understand the advantages inherent in interest rate gyrations. First, as interest rates swing back and forth, the client, has multiple opportunities to obtain rates of interest which are fixed over long periods of time and which may be much higher than the long-term inflation rate. In determining what rates of interest are attractive, it is important for the broker and his client to compare the rates offered to the *long-term* inflation rate rather than the current inflation rate. Second, the price of bonds changes due to the ever-changing interest rates. This event gives the broker's client opportunities for capital gains from interest rate changes as well as from bonds maturing. Consequently, an investor can achieve a substantial total return, comprised of interest income and capital gains. Third, if the investor's timing is poor and interest rates continue to climb, he has opportunities to establish short-term capital losses through "tax swaps." Such short-term losses can be used to shelter investment income from high income taxes while the gain in the new bond will not be taxed until some point in the future when it is

188

sold. When the sale finally does occur, a long-term capital gain will be realized and will be taxed at a lower rate.

Fourth, the investor who invests in bonds of high quality knows that no matter what mistakes in timing he makes in the meantime, he will get all of his capital back when they mature. This last advantage might appear meaningless until the young broker thinks of all the money that investors lose after purchasing marginal, highly speculative securities in search of capital gains.

The quality spectrum of bonds available is similar to equities. Issues run the gamut from "junk" bonds to U. S. Treasury bonds. There are convertible bonds which essentially can become equities to "put" bonds which can become "time out" or "home" bases when the interest rate picture becomes too fuzzy.

Returns on bonds can be significant, particularly if a client uses the leverage available to him. Annual total returns of 30% to 40% are not uncommon. Therefore, it is vital for the young broker to develop an awareness of the mechanics of the bond market and the opportunities awaiting him there.

FWIW # 112 .... A Bond Portfolio

Before a young broker can successfully develop a clientele with substantial bond portfolios, he must plan not only an investment strategy but also a sales presentation. For the young broker, the beauty of this type of investing is that he can use the same sales presentation for all prospects/clients simply by changing from taxable to non-taxable bonds. The approach to be outlined here is especially effective for retirement accounts since those accounts are particularly susceptible to unexpected demands for substantial withdrawals. Finally, the approach outlined below enables the investor to take advantage of changes in interest rates.

Structuring the portfolio begins with determining the age of the investor or investors. For a retirement account, this is the stipulated retirement age of the major participants. The broker adds five years to this predetermined retirement age to arrive at the maximum maturity for the portfolio. For example, if the investor is 50 years old and expects to retire at 65, the maximum maturity used in the portfolio is 20 years. The young broker should exercise caution in believing his prospect/client who says he plans to retire at the age of 55 or less. Many people profess an ambition to retire at such an early age, but very few people actually do so. The broker must make a decision and then persuade the prospect/client of the merits of the decision.

Knowing that the shortest possible amount of time for fixed income/fixed maturity investing is 90 days, and that the longest possible period for such investing is determined by the time left to retirement plus five years, the broker can divide the intervening time into "time groups" of approximately four years. He should allocate a share of the initial capital to each time period at the time he sets up the portfolio. The percentage allocated to each group depends on the individual client. The broker should take care to indentify each known need for funds such as a child going to college or a large loan maturing when setting up the schedule.

The second step in structuring the portfolio has to deal with the direction of interest rates and the shape of the yield curve. The broker allocates funds to every time period and the client's personal circumstances influence that distribution to a degree. If interest rates are going higher and the shape of the yield curve is inverted, more weighting could be given to the short and intermediate maturities until the long maturities reach a certain level. It is important to invest funds in all "time groups" since no one, repeat no one, has the ability to consistently and accurately forecast interest rates.

The third step in structuring the portfolio is to consider the coupon amount of the bonds selected. With wildly fluctuating interest rates, there is a very real dilemma inherent in investing in long-term bonds with good yields which can be called just when an investor does not want them called - i.e., when interest rates are low. It is the broker's obligation to know the call feature of any bond he sells to a client. If the broker is a real professional, he will attempt to gauge the probability of the issue being called in various market scenarios. While there are no guarantees, making a professional estimate is better than giving no thought to the matter at all. To address this potential problem, it is recommended that the broker correlate the maturity schedule with the coupon rate. Since most bonds have call protection for the first ten years, current coupon issues could be purchased for all "time groups" extending as far as ten or twelve years. After twelve years, the broker should use bonds carrying coupon rates ranging from slightly to significantly below current rates. By using this approach, the broker can ensure that the portfolio has some call protection as well as the

MY WAY

191

MY WAY

opportunity for capital gains. For example, if current coupons are 12%, issues to be considered for long maturities could have coupons in the 8% to 10% range. While call protection is important, the investor's personal circumstances and investment objectives are paramount and must be considered.

As stated earlier, other factors, such as the desire or need for taxable or non-taxable income should not influence the portfolio's structure. Nor should quality ratings be considered.

Once the initial portfolio is in place, new funds and income generated can be used to fill in any gaps in maturities so that eventually there are bonds maturing each and every year. The investor's needs, the direction of interest rates, and the shape of the yield curve should continue to influence the weighting of these funds. As the investor grows older and bonds mature, he can extend his time horizon on maturities, or the portfolio will become more compressed until the investor reaches 70 and the retirement account is in a completely liquid state.

If the retirement account is properly designed, 15% to 25% of the investor's bond principal should be invested within the first five years. These funds, which should stay at par or close to par, when combined with the ability to draw emergency funds from a margin account, should give him sufficient liquidity in his portfolio. Every day that he owns the portfolio, a portion of his funds becomes more liquid since all of the bonds come closer to maturity. Current interest income can be reinvested in the most opportune maturity and coupon rate based upon the investor's needs, the current direction of interest rates, and the yield curve.

While it sounds very complex to structure a bond portfolio in this manner it is not. Moreover, the concept is easy to explain to a client in such a way he (1) becomes excited with it, and (2) is impressed with the broker's professionalism. The young broker should have before him a legal pad and pen - nothing else. He should start with a clean sheet of paper and design the concept before the client's very eyes by asking him questions. Here are some appropriate questions:

(1) How old are you?
(2) How old is your spouse?
(3) Do you intend to retire at 65?
(4) Do you intend to use the interest income for expenses now? Later?
(5) Do you see any definite unusual needs for cash in the future?
(6) Do you have in mind a minimum quality rating for the bonds?
(7) Do you prefer taxable or non-taxable income?
(8) What is your tax bracket?
(9) How much capital will be committed to the portfolio?

The list of questions can go on and on. As the client answers each question, the broker should record the information in the upper left hand corner of the blank page. (See Item "A" at end of FWIW) After he has collected the needed information, the broker can explain the three possible shapes of the yield curve by illustrating them in the right hand corner of the page. (See Item "B" at end of FWIW)

Across the middle of the page the broker can sketch the appropriate "time groups" with recommended percentage weightings based upon the

MY WAY

193

MY WAY

investor's needs, the direction of interest rates, and the shape of the yield curve. (For illustrative purposes, a level amount of 20% is shown on the sample page.) Directly below that, the broker should show the coupon amount to be targeted in each category. He could explain briefly, using arrows, to indicate what would happen to each "time group" as interest rates go up or down. He should emphasize the liquidity and flexibility of the portfolio as interest rates go up, and the capital gains potential as they go down.

By utilizing both oral and written communication skills in the sales presentation, the young broker insures his prospect/client will remember it. Under no circumstances, however, should the broker leave the conceptual drawing with the prospect/client. Without it, he will remember the gist of the presentation, but he will not be able to duplicate the plan. If the prospect/client wants to implement the plan, he must use the young broker. The young broker can retain the sketch without offending if he says:

"Mr. (*Name*), rather than leave this sketch with you today, I will send you a typewritten version once you have decided to implement the bond portfolio approach. It will have enough space for you to actually fill in the "time groups" with specific purchases as we find them. Shall we begin constructing the portfolio with $____?"

If the prospect/client is already heavily invested in the bond market, this approach moves the young broker a little closer to getting the opportunity of reviewing his portfolio. After going through the presentation as previously outlined, the young broker could conclude:

"Mr. (*Name*), Wouldn't you like to have your present bond holdings analyzed and listed with "time groups," to see where you are over and under weighted, based upon the direction of interest rates and the shape of the yield curve?"

The beauty of this approach for the young broker is that he sells the concept and not the individual bonds. He need not worry that a particular issue will be gone when the prospect/client finally makes up his mind. Once the investor has committed his funds and the initial portfolio is implemented, the broker presents the client with a very neat and professional spread sheet in a file folder. He instructs the client to keep the folder in his office so that whenever the broker calls him with a recommendation, he will be able to see how the new purchase would fit into the portfolio. It is very hard for the client to turn down a good recommendation when he is staring at written proof the bond is needed. The final advantage to the young broker in developing bond business is bonds have no visible commission. While there is an increasing amount of competition from discount brokers, it cannot hurt the young broker in this area. It is customary for bonds to be placed in inventory and the price adjusted to changes in interest rates. Because there is no visible commission, the young broker is not pressured by the prospect/client to give him a discount. Consequently, competition for the client's business will be based purely upon the professionalism of the broker and attractiveness of the bonds.

MY WAY

"A" Bob Wilson
Age 50 - Wife 48
College costs 10 years & 15 years
50% Tax Bracket
Tax Free Bonds

"B" Yield Curve

Normal   Flat   Inverted

	0 - 4 Years	5 - 8 Years	9 - 12 years	13 - 16 years	17 - 20 years
Allocation of Funds Initially:	20%	20%	20%	20%	20%
Coupon Rates:	Current	Current	Current	Slight Discount	Discounted
Rates Go Up:	—→	→	→	→	→
Rates Go Down:	—↑	↑	↑	↑	↑

Interest Income and New Money invested according to current conditions when funds available.

FWIW # 113 ....Premium Bonds

When interest rates are volatile, there are times when bonds with long maturities sell at prices over par, and in some cases, significantly over par. At some point, the young broker should show his client the benefit of exchanging high premium bonds for a larger amount of discounted bonds. If he does so, the client exchanges higher income now for a known capital gain at maturity. While the argument could be made that the value of the current income is worth more than the future capital gain, the young broker should also keep in mind that interest rates are volatile and that a drop in rates could cause a price change in the discounted bonds before maturity. A call factor could also prevent premium bonds from increasing in price. Moreover, a client usually recognizes the advantage of going from a smaller to a greater quantity of bonds.

FWIW # 114 ....Tax Loss Swapping

There is no better way to enhance the yield of a portfolio than by creating tax losses without really losing anything. Suppose an investor purchases an XYZ 8% bond due in 2000 at par. Sometime later, the bond is selling for $750 since interest rates have moved higher. If he holds the bond until the price returns to par either because interest rates have come down or because the bond has matured, he stands to gain nothing! His broker finds a YZA 8% bond maturing in 2001 selling for $750. By paying a commission, the investor can swap the XYZ bond for this YZA bond and create a tax loss now of $250 per bond. Has he lost anything? He

MY WAY

has paid a commission, probably $10 per bond, but he still has the same number of bonds he began with. When the bonds mature or when the interest rates come back down to the level they were at when he bought the bonds, the investor will get his entire principal back. He has gained significantly through the swap. Depending on his circumstances, he will either (1) save actual tax dollars, or (2) shelter other taxable income. These are very real savings!

The young broker needs to understand that "tax swaps", are not really as simple as the illustration indicates. There are five variables which he must consider in arranging a tax swap:

(1) Number of bonds
(2) Maturity dates
(3) Coupon amounts
(4) Quality
(5) Additional funds needed.

It would be nice if the broker could find two bonds with identical characteristics, but, that rarely happens. Usually, he must change one of the five criteria in order to make the swap work. Maturity is the easiest criterion to change since there is room within "time groups", and very few investors really care whether the bonds they own mature in 17, 18, 19, or 20 years.

Even though bond swaps make a lot of sense, it is the rare broker who makes a point of educating his client in the logic underlying bond swaps. Moreover, neither the typical client nor his broker thinks about doing swaps until the end of the year. Usually the year end is when the demand for swaps is so great that a large number of bad swaps are made simply because time is running out. The professional broker makes tax swapping a part of his daily review every day of the year in order to give his client increased liquidity and flexibility.

FWIW # 115 .... **Options**

Options are wasting assets. Every young broker should be made to write that sentence 10,000 times prior to buying an option for a client. *Options are tools and not assets.* He should also be required to write that sentence 10,000 times.

Many a young broker does great damage to his budding career by getting actively involved in the buying of options for clients shortly after completing his training. He spends the time which he should be using to prospect and develop his investment knowledge trying to make a fast buck for a few under-capitalized speculators. The typical option buyer has $5,000 to $10,000 and dreams of turning it into $100,000 overnight by hitting it big in the option market. This is a fool's game. It is difficult enough to pick a stock which will move substantially higher in price, much less to pick one which will do it in six months or less. Finally, the option buyer is quick to point out the limited risk of buying options. While this statement is correct, he generally fails to point out that the loss is usually "limited" to 100%.

This FWIW is not intended to be a total condemnation of the option markets. It is meant only to remind the young broker of the complexity of the option markets and of his need to study some of the excellent books that have been written on the subject. Until he has done so, he should follow these guidelines:

(1) If a client wants to buy an option, the broker should find one without a time premium. This will probably require the

MY WAY

client to purchase an option which is deep in the money.

(2) When buying an option, the broker should find one with the longest possible maturity. That way, if the price of stock declines, there is the possibility that the option may develop a time premium and, therefore, decline less than the price of the stock. If the stock goes up, the option should track the price increase if it is deep in the money.

(3) The stocks with listed options are generally the most "efficient" stocks. If an option is carrying a large and unusual premium, there is a reason for it. The young broker should never believe the market is giving something away, even if (especially if) his client thinks it is.

(4) The young broker should allow his client to write puts only on stocks he wants to own at prices he is willing to pay. The premium collected becomes very small when the client finds himself the owner of a high priced "dog."

(5) If he is writing a naked call, the young broker should strongly urge the client to put a stop loss order in the market at the same time he takes the position. A young broker and an unsophisticated client can lose so much money so quickly that they never know what hit them until it's all over.

(6) The young broker should not recommend collecting an option premium unless it gives the client twice the current risk-free rate of return.

(7) Computers are mindless. No matter what the statistical number crunching indicates,

a computer printout is no substitute for good judgement and common sense.

MY WAY

FWIW # 116 .... Futures

The best advice than can be given to a young broker is to get completely in or completely out of futures. It is a highly specialized area which has unique rules and which requires intense concentration of efforts to be fruitful. Moreover, brokers who deal in futures must have a special psychological make-up uniquely suited to trading the markets and dealing with the paticipants. A broker who attempts to do both traditional business and futures business takes on unnecessary obstacles to success.

FWIW # 117 .... Limited Partnerships

Real estate and other investment areas with special tax advantages are usually offered to investors in the form of limited partnerships. One advantage that this investment structure has for the client is that it defines his potential loss (100% of the funds put up) while allowing the tax advantages to flow straight on to his individual tax return. A second major benefit lies in the fact that the general partner's expertise is not available to the client in any form other than this one.

The negative aspect of the limited partnership is its lack of liquidity. Most partnerships are designed to be held for at least seven years and to be basicly self-liquidating. Most brokerage firms are now making an effort to market limited

MY WAY

partnerships in the secondary markets, but, the results are usually unsatisfactory. It is imperative for the broker to make his client aware of the illiquidity factor in a professional manner.

In summary, limited partnerships are gradually becoming more popular with brokerage firms as the array of investments offered to the public becomes wider. Consequently, the young broker must communicate to his client all of the ramifications to avoid problems.

FWIW # 118 .... Tax Shelters

Since Congress uses tax laws to move capital into areas where it will enhance the social or economic well being of the country, the nature of "the good" tax shelter changes every time the tax laws change. For this reason, it is imperative that the professional broker keep himself well versed in the intricacies of the tax code. While he must not give tax advice, it is important for him to recognize needs and opportunities that his client may not see. When these occasions arise, the broker should steer the client to his tax advisor with a list of questions designed to bring the investment need to surface. Even better, the broker can ask for the client's permission to talk directly with his tax advisor. This direct communication can help to avert a potentially explosive situation wherein the tax advisor feels threatened. All the broker wants is the sale and not credit for the idea. By assisting the tax advisor in a quite and professional manner, the broker can meet his goal and develop a relationship with the tax advisor which will lead to referrals.

The difficulty in developing tax shelter business lies in the fact that most investors concern themselves with tax planning only around April 15 and at the end of December. Even in April, when high quality tax shelters are readily available, they procrastinate until the year's end, when it is too late to find a good tax shelter for that year. As the laws tighten around tax shelters suspected of being fraudulent, the need for advance planning becomes more and more evident.

Tax shelters take the form of either public or private programs. The law dictates that the client pay for a public program within one year. Some oil and gas programs are designed so that the investor makes payment in the last quarter of a year and the second payment just after the beginning of the next year. This enables the investor to get a "multiple" write-off the first year. Public programs are designed to start giving the investor some of his money back in a relatively short time, usually one and one half to two years. Consequently, the young broker should regard public programs as high risk income spreading programs.

Since the legal definition of "sophisticated" investor has been changed to mean anyone who has a net worth of $1,000,000 or an income of $200,000 per year, private programs have become popular. A young broker should spend his time working on finding investors who have an interest in, and qualify for, these private programs. The young broker can tag a question onto the end of every prospecting call:

"Mr. (*Name*), from time to time my firm has available private placement tax shelters which offer investors multiple writeoffs. To qualify for having the opportunity to review these private

MY WAY

MY WAY

placements, an investor needs to have a net worth of $1,000,000 or an income of $200,000. Would you be interested in a multiple writeoff? (Assume yes). Excellent, let me get some information from you in order to submit your name as a qualified investor when an opportunity arises. There is no obligation, of course."

The broker will get substantial information about the prospect's/client's portfolio as he completes the questionaire for an "Offeree Qualifying Wire." He will also be able to quickly respond to notices of impending opportunities. This speed is necessary since many of these tax shelters are sold within a matter of days.

A tax shelter which offers a multiple writeoff in any given tax year does so by (1) borrowing money to go with the investors' funds, or (2) being designed so as to load the writeoffs all at one time. Consequently, the young broker should find out by what means a program offers a multiple writeoff. He should also remember that the tax laws do not allow a writeoff greater than the amount the investor has at risk. If the program borrows money and then proves to be unsuccessful, someone must pay back the money it borrowed. That someone is the broker's client.

Before recommending a tax shelter to a client, the young broker should ascertain what percentages of his client's money will actually go into the shelter. Fees can take as much as 25% in some shelters. Comparing the fee structure plus the illiquidity of the tax shelter investment to alternative investments, as well as ways to utilize the after tax amount of the funds, will give the young broker and his client a clearer understanding of the shelter's merits as an investment. Along these

same lines, the economic merit of the tax shelter
should be analyzed. The shelter should make good
sense without tax advantages.

In summary, tax sheltered investments do have
a role to play for the right investors, and, as
always, it is up to the broker to match the right
client with the right tax shelter.

MY WAY

FWIW # 119 .... A Secret

The difference between a mediocre broker and
a professional broker is that the mediocre broker
takes a little amount of money and tries to do a lot
with it whereas a professional broker takes a lot
of money and does a little with it.

To be able to handle a lot of money and clients,
a broker must be able to organize his business so
that all aspects flow smoothly and harmoniously.
Getting it all together is only half the battle; the
other half is KEEPING IT TOGETHER.

KEEPING IT TOGETHER

MY WAY

Every transaction completed by a broker must start in one of two ways. Either the broker begins with a client who has an investment want or need, or he begins with an investment opportunity. In order to effectively match investors with opportunities and opportunities with investors, a broker must be organized. This need for organization should guide the young broker in setting up his work area.

The broker should have a desk and a two drawer file cabinet in his work area. If the floor plan of the office does not leave space enough for him to put his file cabinet next to his desk, the young broker should find a place for one somewhere else in the office. While it is a great deal more inconvenient for him not to have his files at his fingertips, the young broker can live with the situation until he earns a private office. Finally, it is recommended that the young broker keep his file cabinet locked and the key in his desk.

FWIW # 121 .... Desk Organization

The way a person organizes his desk is a personal matter. There are, however, some "tricks of the trade" which enable the young broker to transact business more quickly:

(1) Every desk has one or two writing boards which pull out just above the drawers. The broker will find it helpful to have monthly beginning and ending trade dates for each production month taped to this board along with a listing of frequently called numbers.

209

MY WAY

(2) In one of the top drawers on either side the broker should have his (a) commission schedule, (b) telephone book, (c) quote book, (d) compliance guide, and (e) S&P handbook. The compliance guide should be where the broker can't help but see it as he reaches for these other frequently used items.

(3) Most desks have one deep file drawer. The nature of this drawer's contents partially depends on the proximity of the broker's file cabinet to his desk. If it is close enough to be readily accessible, the young broker should keep files on major investment areas in his desk, and (should keep) client and company files in his file cabinet.

Files on major investment areas should contain information explaining the features and benefits of each investment, as well as current available offerings in that area.

(4) One desk drawer should contain order blanks of every nature as well as copies of reported trade tickets for the trailing six months. Trade tickets may also be kept elsewhere since they may be used as a means of tracking long-term or short-term capital gains.

(5) One of the bottom drawers on either side should be used for all of those items which cross a broker's desk and which he is planning to get to "later." Since "later" never seems to come, the broker can simply dump the contents in the trash can whenever the drawer is full.

FWIW # 122 .... Client Folders   *MY WAY*

While the young broker does not have enough
room to maintain a file on each and every one of
his clients, he is a very foolish man if he does not
have one on each of his major clients. The definition of a major client is the same as that of a
serious investor or a guided account (FWIW
77). Within a major client's file should be
copies of every piece of correspondence to or
from the client, every monthly statement, every
inter-office memo on a problem, every deposit
receipt, every check disbursement memo, and
notations of every phone call which the broker
deems to have been of immediate or potential
importance.

The purpose of the file is to provide a complete
history of the account so the broker can accurately reconstruct past events should the need to do
so arise. The only item which should not be in the
file is the account "holdings" page. The value of
the account file is twofold: it enables the broker
to periodically review its history thereby detect-
ing gradual changes in the client's pattern of
investing, and it provides a clear and verifiable
picture of what has transpired.

FWIW # 123 .... Cross-Referencing Clients

Some transactions begin with the broker having
an investment opportunity and looking for a
suitable prospect/client. To reduce the time it
takes a young broker to find those prospects/
clients who have expressed an interest in a particular type of investment, the young broker needs to
develop a system of cross-referencing for his

MY WAY

clients and 300 Club members. Nothing is more frustrating to a young broker than remembering that one of his clients is interested in annuities but unable to remember which one.

The solution to the problem lies in asking the right questions, (FWIW # 67), and then listing each prospect/client on pages in an account book or storing the information on a personal computer. The same cross-reference page used for individual security holdings can be adapted by listing the prospect's/client's phone numbers instead of account numbers. By maintaining these "interest" pages in his account book, the young broker can immediately go to those prospects/clients who have expressed the most interest in the type of investment opportunity available. After the broker has called everyone who has said they were interested in a particular type of security, he should call the rest of his prospects/clients if for no other reason than to be able to offer them a good opportunity. Since he has already made the calls with the greatest potential for being productive, he can use these calls to probe the prospect's/client's investment objectives.

There is a final use for the cross-referencing of prospects/clients. As time goes on, everyone's investment objectives change. Sometimes, the broker is not aware of these changes. By setting up a schedule to send his clients a letter each year, the broker can accomplish three objectives: (1) to thank the client for his business, (2) to get revised and updated investment objectives, and (3) to ask for referrals. The letter could go as follows:

Dear (*Name*):

It has been   years since you did me the honor of becoming my client. This letter is partially to thank you for your business and continued good will. You will find atached hereto a list of investment opportunity categories that our firm handles. When we first started doing business, you indicated a preference for those checked.

In order to give you the opportunity to review all investments of interest; yet, avoid being bothered about non-suitable investments, please review the listing and make any changes that are appropriate. Kindly return it in the enclosed, self-addressed, stamped envelope.

On the same page there is space for you to list anyone you know who may have a need or desire for my services. Thank you again for your patronage and goodwill.

Sincerely,

Sending out the letter on the anniversary of the account opening will help the broker keep on top of his business as well as stimulating referrals.

FWIW # 124 ..... Utilizing the Quote Machine

Only the telephone is more important to a broker than his quote machine. Through the proper use of the quote machine, the broker can maximize his ability to satisfy his prospects'/ clients' investment objectives. A few years ago, a broker could get only quotes on his quote machine - nothing else. Today, most firms communicate not only their entire bond inventory but special investments as well. The quote machine

MY WAY has also become the new means of news disseminating and updating client account records.

Early in the morning, when the terminal has been updated, the broker should review the latest news and determine whether it requires any action from him on his part. Between 9:00 a.m. and 10:00 a.m., he should review all of the information about the investment opportunities currently being offered by his firm.

Shortly after the market opens, around 1:00 p.m., and after the close, the broker should check the price on every stock in which he has a position or interest. In addition, he should look at the market indicators which are available on the terminal.

As a broker begins to produce more business, he should qualify to have monitor lines added to his desk terminal. He should use these lines for market indicators and his five largest equity positions. Monitor lines enable the broker to check the market in just a glance.

The best business generating feature of the desk terminal is its capability to instantly produce complete and up to date information on client's holdings. Having updated information on values and positions gives both the broker and the client the flexibility to aggressively look for opportunities. Another feature is access to the research department recommendations, which enables the broker to intelligently discuss investments without having to constantly hang-up and call back. All of these features add to the broker's professional image.

**FWIW # 125 ..... Improper Use of the Quote
Machine**

The temptation inherent in the desk terminal is that it is interesting to work with and gives instant gratification. If the broker wants to know the price of a security, all he has to do is touch a few keys. If he wants to know what news stories are affecting the market or his stocks, all he has to do is touch a few keys. In some cases, the broker can obtain complex option strategies by keying in the current price of the stock and options. All of these activities are fun and make the young broker look busy. Therein lies the problem. He is busy performing a function other than calling prospects/clients and making recommendations. The desk terminal has the potential to become a major distraction for the broker instead of a valuable tool.

FWIW # 126 .... Today's Opportunities

Because the number of available investments has so greatly proliferated in the last few years, it has become increasingly difficult for the young broker to make sure he is aware of what opportunities are being offered each day. One way for the young broker to have current ideas at hand is to develop and complete a daily list entitled "Today's Opportunities." He should keep this with the bond inventory sheet, (FWIW # 101). The firm's headquarters is usually the main source of the ideas, but other sources could include traders or other merchandising specialists. Whatever his source, the wise young broker makes a note of it so he can remember whom to contact with an order when he gets one.

MY WAY

Since it takes time to methodically review all investments that are available, it is recommended the young broker start as early as possible in the morning.

FWIW # 127 .... Micro-Cassette Recorder

A terrific tool for the young broker is a micro-cassette recorder. It is small enough to be carried in a coat pocket, yet will record for over an hour. It's purpose is to record ideas, insights, and inspirations which strike in places where it is not possible to stop and write them down. The prime time for utilizing the recorder is in traveling between home and office. This is the time when the young broker encounters many businesses, neighborhoods, and potential clients. He can record the names or addresses of residences or businesses which look interesting, and can later check the city cross-reference directory to get a name and address.

Using a micro-cassette recorder does not come naturally. After the novelty wears off, the broker finds himself forgetting to carry it with him. This is when he needs to exercise self-discipline to make the use of the recorder a habit. It must become second nature to him. One way to develop the habit of using it is to set aside a certain time every morning to review what has been recorded and to act upon the information. Successes thus derived reinforce the broker's desire to use the recorder.

The young broker should be a constant fountain of ideas. Once they start to flow, they come too quickly for him to record in written form. The micro-cassette recorder can pay for itself in a few weeks. It will continue to aid the young broker in increasing his professional stature for many years.

MY WAY

FWIW # 128 . Long-Term/Short-Term Control

The young broker who does not have a personal computer can still keep track of when his client's investments will become long-term capital transactions. Each day, a broker receives either copies of his "confirmations of purchase/sale" or a listing of those transactions from the previous day. The typical young broker checks the information for errors and then files it away forever. It is recommended instead that the young broker file this information in an accessible place, in chronological order, with the dates clearly marked.

When planning his day, the young broker should go to his file and pull all of the transactions which are exactly 31 days away from becoming long-term. In other words, if the long-term holding period for an investment is six months, the broker should review the transactions which took place four months and 29 days ago. The young broker should review the transactions to see if his clients have losses on their positions. Since they would be adversely affected if the loss were to become long-term, he should call to recommend replacing the higher priced shares with shares at the current price. To get around the "wash" sale rule and still to take a short-term loss, the client must effect this transaction 31 days prior to the six month holding period. The end result is that the client ends up with the same number of shares as well as a short-term tax loss to offset investment income or capital gains.

MY WAY

FWIW # 129 .... Time Control

While many executives have the ability to tightly control their time partly by means of excellent receptionists, and other "roadblocks", the broker has traditionally been available to his clients at any time and for any reason. That was acceptable when stocks and bonds were all he sold. Today, however, he does not have the time to spend on a wide array of administrative matters. Typically, a professional broker plans his day carefully only to find his plan destroyed by a phone call from an important client who wants a solution to a problem now. This happens frequently because the broker, being a salesman, has never set guidelines with his clients as to his accessibility. In fact, as a young broker, he probably encouraged his clients to call him anytime with questions concerning investments. This policy was suppose to ensure that he would maintain "control" of their accounts. It may have made sense at the time, but now, when he has many clients, he is so busy that he runs the risk of appearing not to care about any of them. This transition is not easy, yet, it is vital if the broker is to grow, and, in the long run, provide better investment ideas to all of his clients.

One of the first things he needs to change is his attitude towards his sales assistant. (The relationship between the broker and the sales assistant will be covered in FWIW # 131.) The broker must shed himself of the long-standing attitude that the sales assistant is nothing more than a glorified clerk. From the very first contact with the client, the broker should make certain he conveys the importance of the sales assistant in the broker/client relationship. Whenever the client brings up a question concerning his account or any other administrative detail, the broker should get the sales assistant on the phone. Next the three of them, client, broker, and sales assistant, should go over the problem. Finally, the broker should then make it clear to the client that the sales assistant will solve the problem and report back to the client. It won't take long before the client is calling the sales assistant directly.

The sales assistant should answer incoming phone calls from all but a small, select group of clients like this:

"Mr. (*Name*) is with a client. May I have him return your call? (either yes or no.) This is Ms. (*Name*), his assistant. If you will explain the nature of the call, Mr. (*Name*) can have the information ready when he calls you back."

The broker can use this information to determine the priority of his call backs. Some merit immediate attention, while others can wait until after the market closes. There are times, of course, when the broker picks up his own phone only to find that a client who wants something of an administrative nature is calling. In this case, the broker should respond:

"Mr. (*Name*), I certainly understand your concern. Let me have Ms. (*Name*) look into this and call you back with an answer by (definite time)."

The broker should set aside certain times each day when he will not take incoming calls at all. All calls during these periods should be outgoing calls where he is either cold calling or asking for an order. These periods are intense, focused, and

MY WAY

219

MY WAY

should last for one to one and one-half hours twice a day.

Since the day an account is opened is the best time to start training a client to respect a broker's time, the broker can make the following presentation then. It works well both with the client on the phone and with the client in person.

"Mr. (*Name*), thank you for opening an account with us. I want to introduce you to my sales assistant, Ms. (*Name*), who handles all administrative functions as well as money market fund orders. If you have any questions concerning your statement or account, please do not hesitate to call (*Name*). Any time you wish to ask questions concerning investments or investment strategy, please don't hesitate to call me directly."

If the broker is already established and needs to wean some clients away from the habit of constantly contacting him with small problems, he can say to them:

"Mr. (*Name*), thanks to good clients like you, my business has grown over the past few years to the point where I am able to have an assistant. From now on, Ms. (*Name*) will assume the function of handling all the administrative areas of my business as well as orders for money market funds. Because she has relieved me of these duties, I will be able to spend more time looking for investments which will offer you potential capital gains."

The last time management problem the broker has to face is keeping other brokers in the office from interfering with his work day. This sounds simple but it is not. (See FWIW # 20) All types of peer problems can arise if the broker is not careful. Other than the last resort of speaking with the manager, the best way to avoid other brokers is to stay busy with a planned day. Any broker who attempts to interfere with another busy broker is insensitive and can be told to go away politely. A nice way of doing it is to say:

"(*Name*), while I do have some calls to make right now, I would like to discuss that with you. Why don't we go at 5:00 p.m. for a quick beer and talk about it then."

More often than not, the other broker will have no interest in discussing the subject after 5:00 p.m. because he will be on his own time then.

Every professional broker knows time is his most precious asset, and it is necessary for him to extract the maximum productivity from it.

FWIW # 130 ..... Using a Personal Computer

Many books have already been written on the personal computer's brokerage applications, and they are only the beginning. As the technology and hardware change, the broker's use of his personal computer also changes. What does not change is the broker's need to clearly understand what he wants the computer to do for him. He should be able to express his objectives in writing before purchasing any equipment.

The first illusion the young broker has about his new personal computer is that it will save him time. In the long run it may, but in the short run he will put more into it than he gets back. The time he saves by adding a function he will spend on operating the system. Whether he decides to

MY WAY

221

MY WAY

purchase preprogrammed software or to program the system himself, he will spend many hours educating himself. Moreover, he must be careful not to take this time away from selling.

The broker's answer to the question "How is this going to help me produce more and become more professional?" should help him to determine both his present needs for his personal computer and the ways in which he will expand those uses in the future.

FWIW # 131 .... Sales Assistant

Just as the nature of the broker's business has changed so have his requirements for and relationship with a sales assistant, (S/A). What used to be "nice to have" has become "need to have," yet, at the same time, scarcer and harder for the young broker to come by. The rising cost of a S/A and the needs and demands of the "super" broker for a registered S/A have left the young broker either sharing one with five or more other brokers or entirely without one. He finds himself in a "Catch-22" in that his manager says he cannot have more adequate S/A help until he produces more, but it is difficult for him to produce more without more adequate help. To compound the difficulty, the S/A assigned to work with the young broker never seems to last long. A tenure of six to nine months is about average.

Since a new S/A accepts the job at the level of pay offered, it would seem that money is not the reason for her leaving within such a short time. There are numerous other reasons for her departure including: broker rudeness, boredom, lack of time control, frustration, and the perception of a deadend job. A major factor contributing to her frustration is the multiple lines of authority over her position. The S/A must answer not only to her brokers, but also to the operations manager, and ultimately to the office manager. Finally, the S/A has been hired at least partly for her organizational skills, and her broker's obvious lack of organizational and managerial skills soon destroys any control she might have had over her time and work flow.

Obviously, the S/A who survives in the position for longer than a year must have some outstanding qualitites which the broker can develop into productive attributes if he is willing to give his time and energy to work with her. If he is going to get himself and his S/A off on the right foot, the young broker must conduct his business on his first day in the same way that he will when his production reaches the million dollar mark. By adopting this attitude, the young broker will avoid the time wasting mailouts and envelope stuffing duties normally assigned to the S/A. He will find more time for selling and she will have more time to work with client account matters. (See FWIW # 129). It is obvious that the young broker's proper use of a S/A leaves both of them with little to do in the beginning. The broker should spend his "free" time prospecting, and the free time for the S/A is available for other brokers.

There are some firms which do not supply S/A help for their brokers. When this is the case, it is up to the young broker to supply his own, since his business cannot grow without administrative help. Rather than go to a temporary help agency, the young broker would do better to hire a housewife with school age children who would

MY WAY

like to work 10-20 hours a week. The reasoning has to do with stability. It takes a while to learn the brokerage business well enough to become effective. If the temporary helper is unavailable after a month, the broker must start training a new one all over again. If he is patient, the young broker can probably find a woman with a college degree who is looking for a position which is challenging but does not conflict upon her family responsibilities. As her children grow up, she will have more and more time to spend working, just at the time the broker's business will demand more and more administrative help. Both parties can benefit from the relationship.

In most firms, however, the young broker returns from training and is assigned to a S/A who works for a whole group of young brokers. His first step should be to take his new S/A to lunch. During this lunch he should suppress his own ego and ask questions to determine his S/A's ambitions, likes, and dislikes. Does she want to get registered? Does she feel her position is a career or a job? What are her plans for a year from now? Five years? The young broker should then explain how he plans to assist her in working toward her goals, in exchange for her help in meeting his. The young broker and the sales assistant should have lunch together every six months to discuss how they are progressing along the paths to their respective goals.

Within the first three weeks, the young broker will know if his S/A has the proper work habits and attitude. If not, the young broker should speak to the manager about being assigned to someone else. Under no circumstances should he get into conflicts with her. Conflicts are counter-productive since they destroy the broker's ability to sell properly.

If the S/A wants to make her position a career and will go about her task with enthusiasm, the young broker should make certain she gets job satisfaction and recognition in return for her services. If the young broker takes pains to utilize the S/A's time productively, he will find that she takes more pride in what she does for him.

One of the first steps a broker should take is to set up an in/out basket system. The S/A puts all of his incoming mail in the "in" basket and nowhere else. All correspondence going out from the broker is placed in the "out" basket. There should be no need to make exceptions. Nor should there be any need for oral explanations of assignments to be done. If the broker cannot reduce his instructions to writing, he cannot communicate them clearly orally. The "out" basket should be emptied by the S/A at least once an hour. She then has the ability to plan her day accordingly. If there is outgoing correspondence to be typed, the broker should have it in the "out" basket no later than by 2:00 p.m. if he expects it to be ready for mailing by 5:00 p.m. Anything put in the out basket after that time should be ready the next day. This in/out basket system allows the S/A a semblance of control over her time and work.

The broker should introduce each new client to the S/A when the account is opened. If the client is in the office, the S/A should be called over, introduced, and the client given a short explanation of her duties as the administrative member of their team. If the broker opens the new account on the phone, the S/A should be brought into a three-way conversation and introduced in that manner. Training the client from the beginning pays off later. The broker can avoid the kind of client disappointment that stems from a drop in

MY WAY

MY WAY

service as his business grows by developing the client's attitude about working with the S/A. This initial client/S/A contact should include the S/A getting all of the new account information and documents. Real responsibility and authority in this area will help her understand the team concept and take a greater interest in her job.

The S/A's secret of success is a file with dividers numbered one through thirty one. Each divider represents a different day of the month. This is the S/A's tickler file. This file relieves her of the need to remember to follow up on anything. By filing her reminders under the appropriate days, she will always know when to follow up. Every bit of work that cannot be completed in one day, or that should be followed up later, goes into this file. Upon arrival in the morning, the S/A simply takes the work out of that day's file and begins.

As discussed in FWIW # 129, the S/A should also be used as a telephone screen for the broker's phone calls.

Very few young brokers realize that there even is a difference between delegating and dumping. Dumping is giving someone a bunch of jobs to do without giving time limits or having follow-up capabilities. Since the broker does not know the work load of the S/A, whom he shares with others, he should allow her to set her own time priorities with reasonable limits. This can be done in a simple written request:

> (*Name*), please make two copies of the 1981 year end statement for John Doe, account 12345. Send one to him and one to his accountant, Harry Wilson, 123 Elm Street, Anywhere, USA., 11122. Let me know if you cannot do this by tomorrow afternoon.

If the S/A responds the task cannot be done by the deadline specified, he should ask her how soon she can get it done. If her answer is acceptable, fine. If not, the broker must look into the situation himself to locate and remove the road block.

The broker and the S/A should have a regularly scheduled weekly meeting at the beginning or the end of the work day. Every pending item she has in her "tickler" file should be reviewed at these meetings. These meetings keep the broker abreast of potential problems and enable him to address the issues before they have time to escalate into crisis resulting in client dissatisfaction and irate phone calls.

Monthly statement time is always a difficult time in a brokerage office because of clients' questions about their statements. In the beginning, before the S/A has developed a good working knowledge of the firm and its accounting methods, the broker and the S/A should sit down together and review each and every monthly statement. This review is important to the broker because it will generate new sales ideas. It is important to both of them because they will be able to spot mistakes and potential problems before their clients do. When "the team" finds one, the S/A should call the client and say:

"Mr. (*Name*), this is (*Name*), Mr. (*Name*)'s assistant at XYZ Brokerage Firm. In reviewing your monthly statement yesterday, we found an error on (date). We are calling you to let you know we are taking care of the problem. I expect to have it resolved by (date), and will call you at that time. Thank you for doing business with us, and have a nice day."

MY WAY

227

MY WAY

This policy of calling the client before he calls the broker will save time and help create more business because: (1) the client is impressed with the account service, (2) the client does not call at an inopportune time, and (3) the client's perception of the S/A's administrative role is reinforced. Once the S/A has gained sufficient experience to know what to look for, she should go through the monthly statements herself looking for errors. She should make notations as to what is being done, thus, when the broker reviews the statements for sales ideas, he is made aware of her corrective action.

In the line of sales help, the young broker can also assign his S/A the function of daily checking ten prospect names against the office account list. When she does the checking is irrelevant, just as long as she gives him ten new cold-call names a day. The other five names to make the 15 necessary will be available from previous days. Knowing the people he is calling are not presently office accounts will greatly enhance the broker's prospecting productivity.

As the S/A becomes more important to the broker's production, the question of the broker's compensating the S/A arises. Since the typical broker has not had any experience in this area, his awkward attempts end in disaster. A young broker who is doing less than $150,000 in production and who shares his S/A with several other brokers should not compensate her, other than a semi-annual lunch, a small birthday present and Christmas gift, and sending her flowers during National Secretaries' Week. At times when she expends extraordinary effort in his behalf, it would be a nice gesture to give her a box of candy. The key is to recognize and encourage.

When the broker considers giving cash pay-
ments, there are two prerequisites. First, the S/A
must be registered. Second, the size of the bonus
must be tied in some way to production levels.
The S/A should not expect a bonus in a year
when production has fallen. At the same time, she
must be able to anticipate a reward for extra
effort in a year when production has risen dramatically. Any financial arrangement between
the broker and S/A must be reviewed and approved by the office manager prior to being put
in writing. While the main criterion must be
production level, there are other considerations as
well:

(1) The effectiveness of the S/A relieving the
    broker of inconsequential client communi-
    cation.
(2) The level of extensions, document controls,
    and problem solving successes.
(3) Level of production generated by small
    accounts serviced solely by the S/A.

Using the broker's total production level as a
guide, the actual amount of the S/A's compen-
sation can be expressed as a predetermined percentage of the total, deducted by the firm from
the broker's commissions and paid to the S/A
monthly. A final word about the amount: Everyone has difficulty in maintaining enthusiasm when
goals have been set either too high or too low.
There is no one right answer since each situation
is unique. To be meaningful for the S/A, however, the amount should increase her gross com-
pensation by at least 15%.
    It is important to mention one final point about
the broker/S/A relationship. The S/A will adopt

MY WAY

MY WAY

work habits and attitudes similar to those of her brokers. If the broker becomes overly familiar with his S/A and breaks down the professional relationship, he will find it difficult to reestablish it. The value of the working relationship should be recognized as more important than any other type.

FWIW # 132 .... The Score

In order to maximize his potential, the young broker must pay attention to his production level every minute of every day. However, this constant awareness of his production level should never conflict with the broker's primary obligation to serve the needs of his clients. His awareness of his current position will prompt the broker to seek out each and every opportunity that presents itself. Before leaving the office each day, the young broker should post on his desk diary his production for the day, week, month, and year to date. He should know where he stands in relation to his performance at the same time last year and his planned goal for the current year.

A goal-oriented person like the broker can always devise games to play with his goals. Sometimes he might work a goal backward. That is to say, start with a total, for instance $50,000, and then deduct his production from it daily until he ends up with zero on the last day. At other times, he might decide to review his client and prospect lists in search of those who are in a position to purchase 2,000 shares of a stock he feels should be positioned. The broker would then spend the major portion of his day calling those people.

Some say a broker should not dwell on production numbers. These critics are usually not goal-oriented themselves, and, they, therefore, do not realize that a truly professional broker has ethical standards which do not permit any "cheating," such as churning or improper investing, merely to enable him to reach a quota.

MY WAY

FWIW # 133 .... Paper Machine

An almost unbelievable amount of paper crosses the broker's desk each day. He would get absolutely nothing done if he stopped to read everything carefully. If he does not develop a system for controlling the paper right from the start he will not progress in his career.

The first step in controlling the paper is to separate it into two piles. The first pile in entitled "nice to know" and the second is "need to know" Once he has sorted the material, the young broker should throw away the "nice to know" information, and should review the "need to know" information on the spot. The broker should either put it in the investment category folders, (See FWIW # 121), or act upon it. He should not read anything that is over one page in length. If a piece is really too important to be thrown away, the broker should take it home to read after dinner.

FWIW # 134 .... Time Out

There are few certainties in a broker's life, but one is that he has one of the best careers on earth. His income level is determined solely by his own efforts, the atmosphere at work is always chang-

MY WAY

ing, and he can spend his whole life in the business and still learn something new everyday. It is a thrilling and challenging way of life, even in the difficult times of bear markets. It is addictive. It quickly gets into the young broker's blood and becomes the central focus of his life.

To be able to enhance this all consuming career, the young broker should develop the habit of setting aside time each day to do nothing but sit quietly and think. He will find this time relaxing and important to his overall understanding of life as well as the dynamics of the markets. If the only difference between humans and other animals is the ability to think and to reason, humans have an obligation to their Creator to develop this special power entrusted to them. Moreover, development of his mental faculties will give the broker the self-confidence to believe in himself. He should review what he has done each day in light of the standards he has set for himself and should take steps to eliminate any discrepancies between the two.

MY WAY NOTES

MY WAY NOTES

MY WAY NOTES

MY WAY NOTES

MY WAY NOTES

MY WAY NOTES

MY WAY NOTES

MY WAY NOTES